UNDERGROUND THANET

Rod LeGear

2012

© Rod LeGear

First published 2012

Trust for Thanet Archaeology
The Antoinette Centre, Quex Park,
Birchington, Kent, CT7 0BH
www.thanetarch.co.uk

© Rod LeGear, 2012

The right of Rod LeGear to be identified as the Author of this work has been asserted in accordance with the Copyrights, Designs and Patents Act 1988.

All rights reserved. No part of this book may be reprinted or reproduced or utilised in any form or by any electronic, mechanical or other means, now known or hereafter invented, including photocopying and recording, or in any information storage or retrieval system, without the permission in writing from the Trust for Thanet Archaeology.

ISBN 978 0 9576512 0 3

Printed by Book Printing UK
Remus House, Coltsfoot Drive, Peterborough, PE2 9BF

Contents

Acknowledgements	6
Underground Thanet	8
Chalk for Agriculture	10
Chalk for Lime Burning	13
Chalk for Brickmaking	26
Thanet at War	30
Transport	57
Enigmatic Sites	63
Smuggling	73
Extended Sea Caves	76
The Future of Underground Thanet	81
Appendix	82
End Notes	84
Further Study	85
Index	86

Acknowledgements

In compiling this brief look at subterranean Thanet the writer must thank the following for their knowledge, photos and surveys without which this paper would be considerably shorter: Angelique Harwood, Vince Runacre, Paul Wells and Barry Stewart. Thanks to Sophie for help with some of the graphics and thanks also to Emma Boast and Ges Moody of the Trust for Thanet Archaeology. All photographs not individually acknowledged are by the writer.

Cover Photos: Front: World War 1 shelter at Ellington School, Ramsgate (© Barry Stewart and KURG). Back: Margate Caves © Rod LeGear

Underground Thanet

The Isle of Thanet is extremely rich in historical and archaeological sites which include a large number of underground features.

The action of the sea on the chalk cliffs which surround most of the island has formed a number of natural caves over the years but the quantity of man made caves and tunnels under Thanet vastly exceeds those formed by nature.

Most of these artificial caves were dug for eminently practical purposes. There are only two basic reasons for digging tunnels and caves underground: either to extract something, i.e. mining for a useful mineral, or to create a functional space for such uses as shelter, storage or the conveyance of people or goods. A good example of the latter type is the 'Seaweed Tunnel' at Pegwell Bay (TR 356 644) which was dug to provide an easy way up to the cliff top fields for farmers who were collecting seaweed to use as a fertilizer.

© *Nick Catford*

In a short publication such as this it would be impossible to note all the underground sites on the island. The following selection represents the varied types of man made underground features that have been recorded by members of the Kent Underground Research Group over many years.

As Thanet is built on underlying chalk it is not surprising that it is this material that has been dug out in vast quantities from both simple shallow pits and larger and more extensive chalk mines.

Raw broken chalk has been used as a fertiliser from very early times. When chalk is burnt it produces lime for lime mortar, lime wash and whiting. Later it was used as a flux in the brickmaking process to produce the characteristic Victorian yellow stock bricks. The chalk was dug from open-cast pits and also from underground galleries entered by either vertical shafts or horizontal entrances from quarry faces.

In 1888 Her Majesty's Inspector of Mines visited an area of **Ramsgate** shown on early Ordnance Survey plans as Hollowcombe Down and reported:

> *"The working of chalk by caves or bell pits in the neighbourhood of Ramsgate having been brought under my notice, I have visited the place and I find that the caves, which have been worked at Hollicondane, extend a short distance underground, and not beyond the daylight; and that the pits worked by windlass are only small shafts, widening out toward the bottom in the form of a bell, similar to some limestone pits in Sussex, and do not require artificial light, so that in neither instance can they be properly classed as mines"*

In the First World War some of the caves in this area were enlarged and used as air raid shelters.

Note: Underground features can be hazardous and many sites included here could only be accessed by experienced investigators using specialist equipment. Great care should always be taken when entering any cave or tunnel. Some coastal caves are cut off at high tide so a check on local tide tables is essential when looking at sea caves.

Many of the sites featured have since been filled or permanently sealed. Sites that are still accessible are on private or local authority land and permission must be obtained before visiting. The exact locations of some sites have been withheld at the owner's request.

Chalk for Agriculture

Small vertically shafted mines were given the name 'deneholes' by Victorian antiquarians, although the term 'chalkwell' can also be applied, especially to those dug from the 17th century onwards. In these small mines the chalk was loaded into a basket at the working face and pulled up to the surface from that point, thus the chambers of these deneholes are quite short as the length of the mined gallery was limited by the friction of the hauling rope on the roof at the shaft bottom.

One such denehole of possible Roman date was discovered between **Northdown** and **St Peters** by workmen digging brickearth in Mr Reeve's Brickfield in February 1876.[1] A small cave was uncovered 3.7m (12ft) down a narrow shaft that penetrated into the chalk. A description by the investigator, George Dowker FGS, states:

> *"The cave was oven-shaped, flat at the bottom, and domed at top, the crown of it being about six feet in height, the breadth of it twelve feet, and the length nine feet."* (1.8m x 3.7m x 2.7m)

Roman pottery, including a piece of Samian ware and an amphora handle, a quern stone and a brass coin of Faustina the Elder were found together with the bones of several animals. The shaft continued down past the cave to a depth of 9.1m (30ft), which is unusual, but not unique. After the examination the shaft and cave were backfilled and made safe.

The location of this denehole is now under Victoria Avenue at TR 3806, 6953.

From a Sketch Plan of 1781

A much larger excavation was being made around 1740 by a certain William Troward who was digging horizontal tunnels near **Manston** village to obtain chalk to mix with manure to use as a fertilizer. Unlike the small chambers of a denehole, the Manston Caves, as they became known, were quite extensive with a network of galleries leading from one or two entrance passages in a shallow quarry face. The chalk was worked in a 'pillar and stall' (or 'pillar and room') system where galleries are dug at right angles to each other leaving square or rectangular pillars of unworked chalk to support the ground above.

Troward was described as: *"...an eccentric bachelor..."* who was known for his good works for the poor.

The site seems to have had unrestricted access after mining ceased and was well known in the area, as by 1781:

> *"...they were much frequented of late by parties who brought their wine and provisions hither in order to enjoy this cool retreat'"*

The entrance to the caves had been carved into an elaborate arch of ecclesiastical proportions, an unnecessary but rather pleasing addition to a simple chalk mine. This was probably viewed locally as proof of Troward's eccentricity.

As with many chalk mines in Thanet, Troward excavated his tunnels too near the surface with insufficient roof cover to prevent frost and rain damage. Consequently, by the late 1780s, a large portion of the caves had fallen in. A sketch of the entrance was published in 1812 which suggests that they were still open at that time but after a few years more serious falls occurred and the entrance became blocked.

The caves get a brief mention in the 'Ingoldsby Legends' where they were said to be the abode of 'Smuggler Bill' but:

> *"Of late they say*
> *It's been taken away,*
> *That is, levell'd and filled up with chalk and clay,*
> *By a gentleman there of the name of Day."* [2]

This would suggest that the site was completely covered by 1840 when the first edition of the Legends was published.

No trace of the caves or the quarry in which they were sited remains. The 19th century descriptions of: *"In a field by the side of the road at the extreme end of the village by a small farmhouse is a cavern called Manston Cave"* is somewhat vague, but a study of old maps and plans could place the quarry at around TR 344 657, inside the boundary of Kent International Airport, just to the west of Bush Farm. Modern maps and aerial photographs show no indication.

In 2002 a subsidence occurred in a field 1.8Km north east of **Manston** village at TR 3348 6737. The collapse revealed the remains of a small agricultural chalk mine of similar age to the Manston Caves. Only one 7.7m long gallery was accessible which was 2.1m high and 1.4m wide at the base with a Norman arch profile. Like the Manston Caves it had been dug very near the surface with the roof only 1.0m below the top of the chalk strata with 0.5m of overlying Clay with Flint deposit giving a roof cover of a mere 1.5m

Several dates between 1751 and 1755 and the initials WI and WT had been carefully carved on the walls, the area being specially smoothed first.[3]

Chalk for Lime burning

Chalk to burn for lime has been dug from numerous small, and some not so small, open pits or quarries throughout the Island. A disadvantage of an open pit is that a large area of land is rendered unavailable for any other use. By digging tunnels from the quarry faces chalk could still be obtained without extending the open pit's boundaries and there are numerous examples of this open and underground working, most of which are simple short galleries dug into the quarry side.

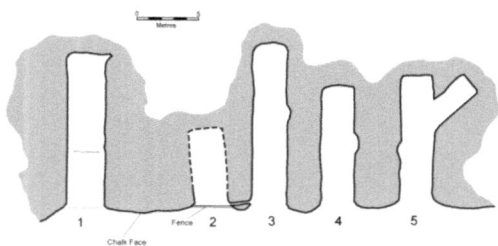

In 1994 two members of KURG visited one such example in the grounds of a house in Elmwood Avenue, **Kingsgate**.[4] The resulting survey by Paul Wells and Andy Miles shows five tunnels around 3.5m high and between 3.0m and 2.5m wide.

The investigators concluded that at least two of the adits (nos. 3 and 4) were dug for lime burning and the others were either dug for, or adapted to, use as an ammunition magazine in the First World War for the nearby coastal guns. Ordnance Survey maps of the area from the 1870's show the quarry as 'Old Chalk Pit' indicating that the excavation and lime burning operation had ceased some time before.

Other quarry tunnels became more elaborate with joining cross passages and many were extended and adapted after chalk mining for other uses such as storage space, and as protection in both World Wars.

One set of tunnels leading from an old quarry near **Ramsgate** was surveyed by the University of Kent Troglodytes Caving Club in 1985 and labelled: 'The Six Mile Mine'. Access to the site was from a private property on Honeysuckle Road.

Seven years later the tunnels were re-surveyed by a KURG team on 14th March 1992.[5]

Originally at least four entrances had been worked from the base of an open quarry face. At the time of the KURG survey only one remained open, the others having been deliberately blocked. The accessible entrance had been re-opened by the owner by digging out a previous attempt to seal the opening. The entrance used in the 1985 survey is now one of those blocked with rubbish and debris.

The plan shows the layout of the tunnels which are typical of the galleries of a small chalk mine dug to provide the raw material for lime-burning. When the open quarry ceased excavation because of boundary limitations, chalk was obtained from the above workings to supply the lime kilns which are clearly shown in the quarry floor on the 1872 O.S. plan.

The galleries had been dug on one level and averaged 1.7m high and 0.8m wide. A large number of candle niches had been cut in the walls, some of which had a small carved slot into which the candle would fit. From the positions of these lighting ledges it is not fully clear whether all of them were cut to light the mining operations or some were constructed at a later date, probably when the tunnels were used as an air-raid shelter in both World Wars.

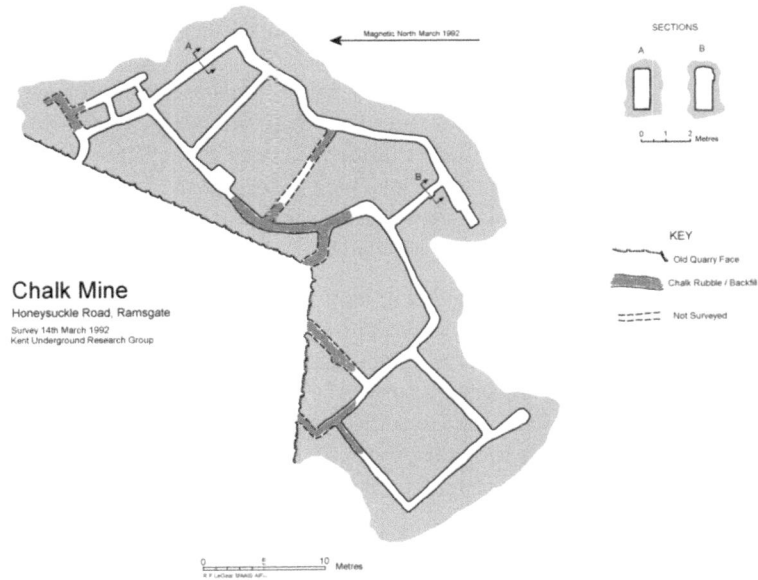

The heights of the galleries show that they were dug after the open quarry stopped production. In many other quarries on Thanet which have associated tunnels they were dug at the same time as the quarry floor descended and are much higher.

© *Angie Runacre*

It can be seen from the survey that the mine consists of small narrow galleries with large areas undeveloped. There has been no attempt to increase efficiency by cutting larger adits or mining on a 'pillar and stall' plan like the Manston Caves. The workings were made by one or two men digging small, man sized tunnels to provide material to keep at least one of the lime-kilns in operation as the business declined.

The mine was named Six Mile Mine at the time of the 1985 survey as there seemed to be some very optimistic speculation that the workings could be much more extensive. The result of the 1992 survey and investigation does not, however, support this view. The only possible extension to the plan would be from the blocked passage to the north of the present entrance. It is far more probable that this just led to another entrance now sealed and obscured by modern buildings.

Similar quarry / underground chalk working have been noted at many locations on the Island, especially around Manston and Acol. Those at

Alland Grange were surveyed by KURG in 1995 and revisited by a small team shortly before they were to be permanently sealed by the farmer in 2009. (See below p27)

On the 8th February 2011 KURG members visited the site of an old chalk pit in the grounds of **Quex Park** near Birchington.[6]

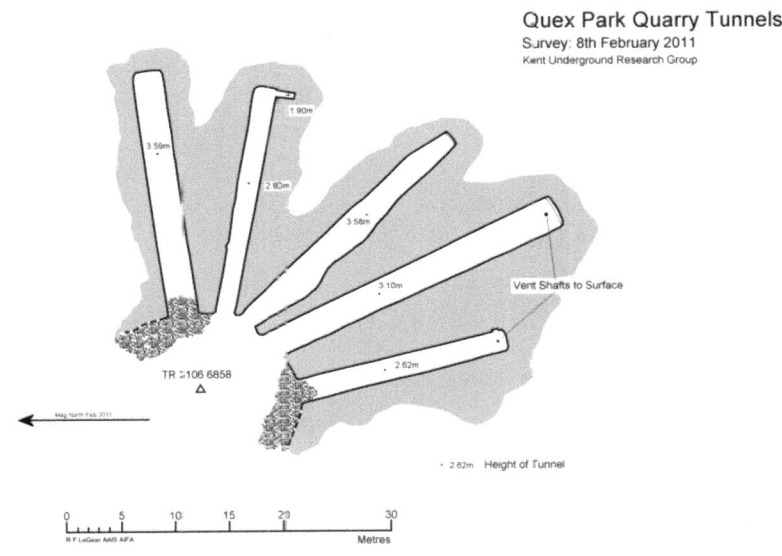

Whilst the pit is noted on the Kent County Council Historic Environment Record (HER) as a post mediaeval chalk pit, the associated tunnels were not recorded.

For some time the pit had been used as a refuse tip so that much of the original layout of the site is now obscured by fill. It was known from old photographs that at one time at least five large tunnels ran from the quarry face, although, due to the in-fill, only three have been visible for a number of years. On the day of the KURG visit access to two other tunnels was gained by digging through debris which had completely covered the entrances.

The five separate galleries were surveyed and the resulting plan shows that whilst the entrances are quite close together, the passages radiate outwards like the spokes of a wheel, leaving large baulks of unworked chalk between them for stability.

All of the caves examined bear considerable numbers of tool marks which show they were dug with standard picks and not a miner's short-headed pick. There is evidence, in the form of slot holes in the walls to support timber beams, that wooden partitions had been erected in some of the tunnels.

It is probable that post excavation the caves were used as convenient storage space for agricultural use and possibly livestock. It is also possible that they were used for mushroom growing at some time in the past.

The quarry is marked on the early O.S. maps of 1871-1890 as 'Chalk Pit' and also shows an associated Lime Kiln whereas the 1897-1900 versions note the site as 'Old Chalk Pit' and 'Old Limekiln'.

Hazel Basford, the archivist at Quex, has found references to the lime kiln in accounts of the 1820s and the pit is noted in an estate terrier of 1834, so it is likely that quarrying and lime burning were in operation from the early 19th century and had been abandoned by the 1890s.

The mansion at Quex Park was built in 1808 with two wings added in 1883. It is highly probable that chalk from the site described above was burnt for lime and used to produce the lime mortar used in the construction.

The old O.S. maps show that the area of the open pit was relatively small and the amount of chalk excavated from the galleries probably exceeded that obtained from the quarry.

The method of working was that the passages were dug as the quarry deepened, i.e. they were dug at the same time as the pit. It would appear that the intention was to obtain most of the chalk from the underground galleries to minimise the size of the open pit.

A good example of a small chalk mine dug from a vertical shaft is the **Margate Caves**, once a popular tourist site. The caves are located at the western end of Northdown Road near Trinity Square at NGR TR 3572 7114.

Unlike a denehole the galleries are quite long indicating that some form of barrow must have been used to transport the chalk from the working faces to the shaft bottom.

The mine was almost certainly dug for lime burning and agricultural use, probably in the late 17th to early/mid 18th centuries.

In the latter half of the 13th century, a gentleman named Francis Forster built a large red-brick house on the site which he called Northumberland House, reputedly after the county where he was born.

Forster's gardener discovered the caves in 1798 when the ground gave way beneath him whilst digging in the garden behind the building. One account of the discovery stated that he died from the injuries sustained falling into the caves.

The subsidence had been caused by the failure of the brick capping over a deep shaft. Following the discovery of the caves Forster started to adapt the underground space for his own use. A stairway was dug into the caves from his rear garden as an easier and safer access than the vertical shaft. Forster was known to be a rather eccentric character and engaged a local artist named Brazier to create some carvings and to paint the various figures and scenes on the chalk walls that can still be seen today. Forster is known to have used parts of the caves for storage, a wine cellar and as a personal grotto

After his death in 1835, subsequent owners of Northumberland House ignored and neglected the caves until, in 1863; they were rented by a shopkeeper from nearby Cecil Square, John Norwood, who opened them to the public for the first time under the name of Vortigern's Cavern. Lighting was provided by sconces in the walls. For a time the site was quite popular but after a few years the enterprise foundered, the site closed and the entrance stairway was filled-in with rubble and rubbish much of which spilled into the galleries.

Several years later the western half of Northumberland House was converted into the vicarage for Holy Trinity Church which had been newly constructed nearby. Dr Prior, the vicar, developed a great interest in the caves and in 1907 re-opened the old entrance stairway and started

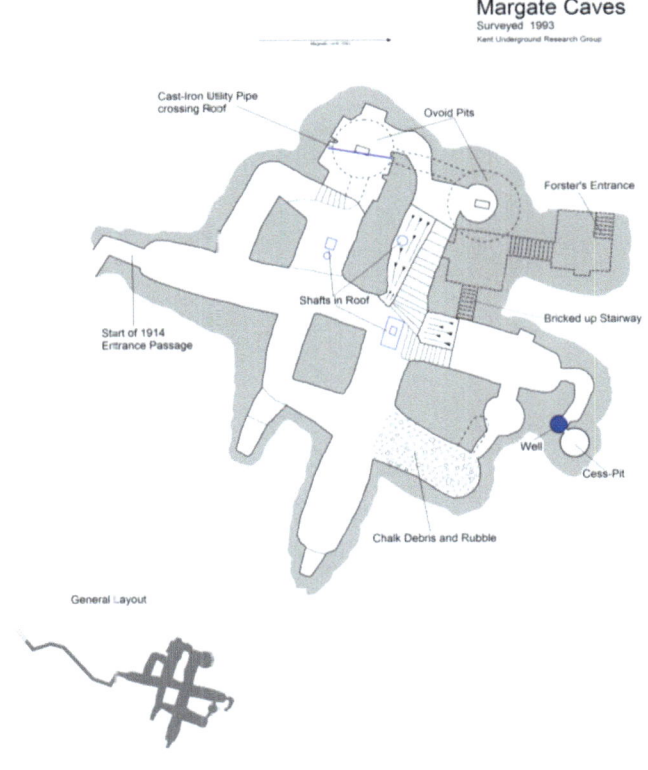

clearing out the debris from the caves. He also cut a small access passage to connect two oval chambers that later became known as 'dungeons'. The enterprising cleric opened the caves to the public in 1910 whereupon they quickly became a popular Margate attraction.

In 1914 a sloping passage was cut from the cellars of the vicarage so that the incumbents could quickly gain the safety of the caves during the air raids of World War I. The general public were allowed access through the 'tourist' stairway in the vicarage garden.

After the First World War the caves were re-opened for tourism until 1938 when they were closed again as the area was scheduled under a scheme called 'The Zion Place Re-development Plan'.

At the outbreak of the Second World War the caves were again used as an air-raid shelter for the vicarage.

In June 1941 both Northumberland House and Holy Trinity Church were destroyed by enemy action. During site clearance the entrance stairs were bricked up where they entered the northern gallery of the caves and then backfilled with rubble to the surface. The site of the vicarage and church were levelled and left more or less derelict for several years.

In the spring of 1958, James Geary Gardner, the proprietor of Chislehurst Caves and other underground tourist caves in the county, became interested in the site and sought to locate a way into the caves. A concrete paving slab in the old vicarage gardens was lifted which exposed the top of Forster's old entrance stairway. This was cleared of rubbish and rubble and the caves were once again made accessible. Having gained access, Gardner enlisted the help of students from the Margate School of Art to clear the blocked 1914 entrance of rubble and debris. A set of modern covered steps was constructed from the surface to reach the chalk entrance passage and two wooden huts for use as a ticket office and gift shop were erected. The caves once again opened to the paying public.

Sometime after Northdown Road was widened and the site came into the ownership of the local authority through a compulsory purchase order. A succession of lessees ran the attraction. A fuller report on Margate Caves can be found on the Kent Archaeological Society's website.

In 2004 the caves were closed due to Health and Safety concerns and at the time of writing (2012) there is a vigorous campaign by Thanet residents to have the remedial work done so that the caves can re-open. This follows Thanet District Council's application for planning permission to build a small housing development on the front of the site which would involve filling the entrance passage with concrete. The Friends of Margate Caves run an excellent web site which gives more information and the latest news: www.margatecaves.co.uk

Another chalk cave was discovered near Margate Caves in October 1959 under the site of some 17th century cottages known as Flint Row.[7] The cottages had been demolished the previous year to prepare the ground for the erection of a three story 'L' shaped block of apartments to be known as Flint House.

The site is located on the southern side of the road opposite Margate Caves which lie approx. 100m to the north. Reports of the discovery stated that a manhole had been lifted which revealed a domed chamber 26ft (7.9m) deep and 36ft (10.9m) across with several tunnels leading off. All of the tunnels were said to be blocked after a short distance. The cavities were filled in and made safe prior to the building works. A plan and section of the feature was unearthed by the curator of the Powell Cotton Museum at Quex Park, Hazel Basford, who kindly allowed the writer to examine it in September 2009 – almost exactly 50 years since the plan was originally drawn up.

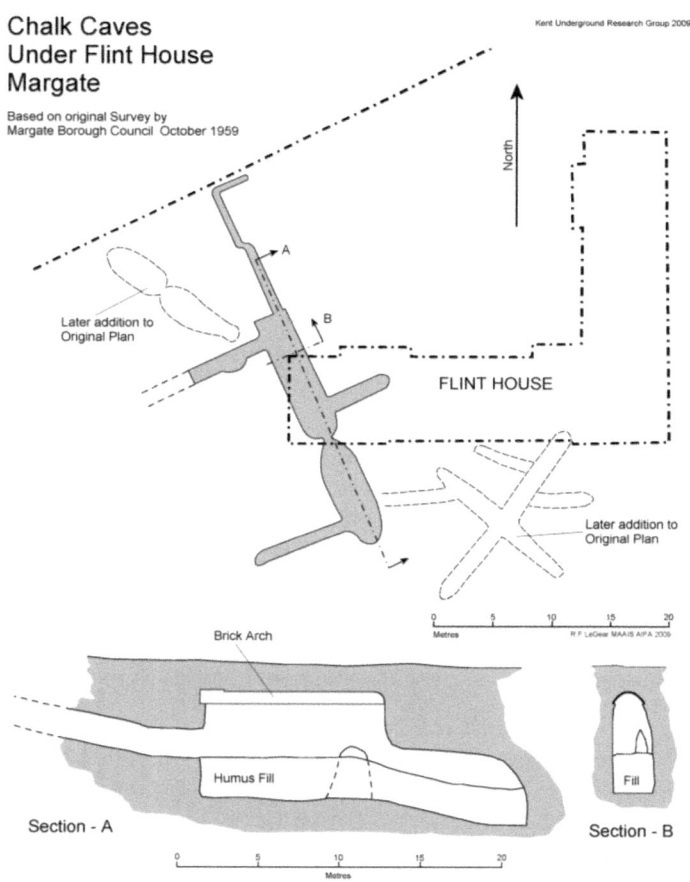

The drawing is titled *'Flint Row Flats, Caves Under Site'* and dated October 1959. It was prepared by the Margate Borough Engineer and Surveyor, George E. Sewell AMICE.

At some time after the drawing was plotted the sites of other nearby cavities had been pencilled in. It is presumed that these were the sites of known caves or that they were subsequently found as ground-works progressed.

The accompanying plan has been prepared from digital photos taken of the Museum copy.

The layout of the caves suggests that they may have been excavated in the First World War as an air-raid shelter. A great number of these were dug in various locations in and around the town, often by inexperienced volunteers. The locations of many are now lost. Another possibility is that an existing cave was adapted as a shelter by the addition of the small northern passage which has a classic anti-blast dog-leg.

In the early 1980s excavations for the foundations of a development at Anvil Close, **Birchington** uncovered the roofs of two sets of chalk tunnels at a depth of 3m below the surface. Members of the Isle of Thanet Archaeological Society dated them to around the 1830s and the theories expressed as to their origin ranged from a buttery to an ice store. The plans suggest that it is much more likely they were dug to extract chalk for lime burning or agriculture.[8]

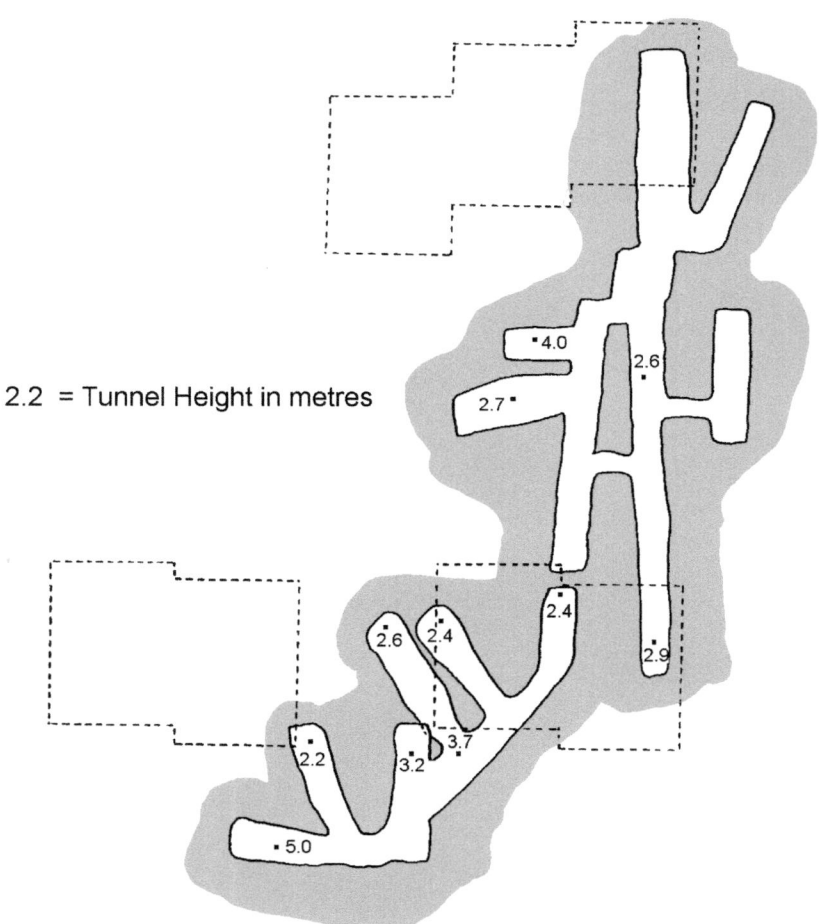

2.2 = Tunnel Height in metres

Chalk for Brickmaking

In the latter half of the 19th century, a large number of brickfields were in operation to supply the growing demand for building materials for the expansion of towns following the coming of the railways. These brickfields sprang up almost anywhere that a suitable clay or brickearth could be found in order to produce the distinctive yellow stock bricks which are such a part of our Victorian townscapes.

The ingredients of the stock bricks produced by these works consisted of brickearth, finely crushed chalk and sifted ashes or breeze. The ashes were obtained from town refuse (an early example of recycling) which was added to the clay and chalk mix so that the raw, or 'green', bricks contained combustible material. The addition of chalk to the mix reduced the tendency for the freshly moulded bricks to crack and shrink when drying. During firing the chalk formed a silicate of lime, which made for a very durable, yet cheaply produced product. The usual amount of chalk added was between 15 and 20%; below this figure the distinctive yellow colour was not achieved. The chalk was obtained as close as possible to the works, from a local quarry if it was practical and economic to do so. It was much more common, however, to win the chalk from a mine sunk in the floor of the brickearth pit. A deep subsidence in a plot of land to the south of Albion Road, **St Peter's** in February 2001 was caused by the collapse of the roof of a large chalk mine associated with a Victorian brickworks.

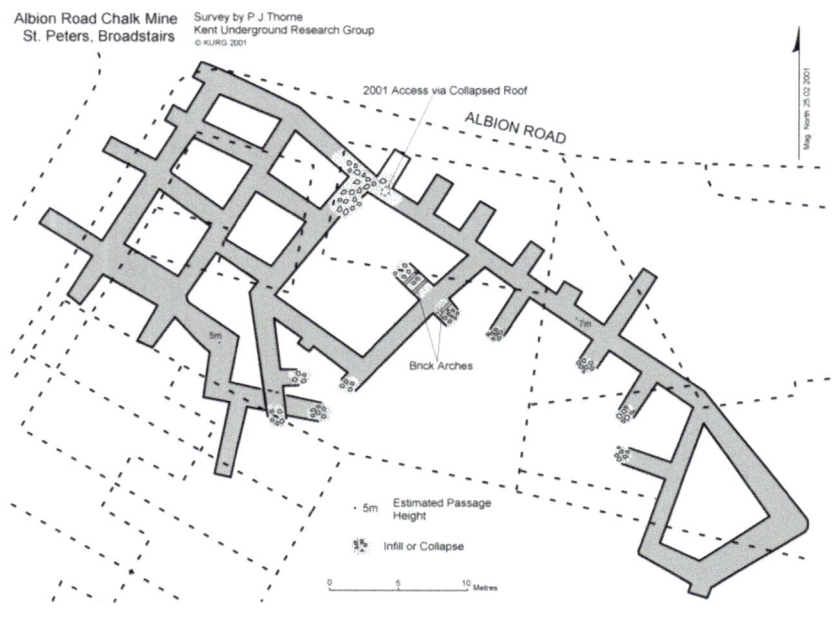

The Kent Underground Research Group was asked to investigate the site and their survey shows that the galleries were excavated with an average width of 2m and were up to 7m high in places. This profile had put high loads on the walls, particularly at passage junctions, and there was evidence of many falls with several cracks visible throughout the mine. There was also evidence, especially in the western tunnels, of water ingress, the walls being stained with soil/Brickearth. At a number of places the excavators had ignored wise mining practise and had driven headings under previously dug tunnels.

At one point, a miner's discarded boot and a pick were found in-situ on a narrow bench of chalk in what was probably the last part of the mine to be worked.

In the summer of 1972 the late Dave Perkins made a brief examination of a hole that had been discovered at Northdown Hill, **St Peters**. In what had once been an overgrown orchard surrounding a derelict bungalow a hole had suddenly appeared beneath the wheel of a mechanical digger that was clearing the area prior to development.

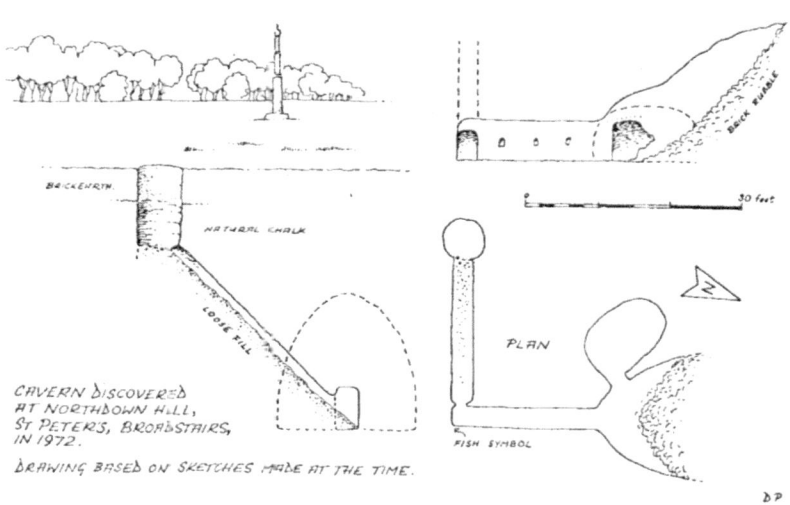

Describing the site in an article in 'Bygone Kent' he states:

> "We found a vertical shaft about 6ft (1.8m) across, descending through the brickearth to a depth of 11ft (3.3m). At this point it went off at a slant through a small opening whose arch was natural chalk..." [9]

After descending what appeared to be a sloping gallery filled to within 2ft (61cm) of the roof with soil and debris:

> "At the bottom we turned right angles into a well cut passage, 6ft by 3ft (1.8m x 0.9m), its surfaces bearing neat pick marks. Our torches disclosed a series of niches cut into the walls, their tops blackened with soot from lamps or candles. After 20ft (6.1m) the passage broke into a cavern, apparently about 20ft (6.1m) high. This was blocked by a great heap of brick rubble which seemed to continue up through the roof. A likely explanation was given later: bomb damage rubble was dumped there in 1940 'to fill a hole that came in the field'. Immediately to the left of the passage opening, another entrance led into a smaller chamber, about 12ft by 8ft (3.6m x 2.4m), and 7ft (2.1m) high".

The location of the shaft was given as NGR TR 3810 6965. The caves were filled in and now lie beneath a road.

At the time of the examination no firm conclusions were reached as to the origins of the chalk caves. The old orchard was, however, situated on made up ground which had once been Reeve's Brickfield. (See page 10) It is therefore likely that the caves described above were once part of a larger chalk mine associated with the brickfield.

Thanet at War

The First World War saw the beginning of a new type of warfare: aerial bombardment from the sky. Being so close to the continent Thanet made a convenient target and consequently suffered many attacks from German Zeppelins and from 1917, Gotha bombers.

In 1917 the local authorities in Thanet held joint discussions that resulted in civilians being asked to volunteer to help with digging shelters.[10]

At Ramsgate a number of large 'dug-outs', as the shelters were called at the time, were constructed in various parts of the town together with the adaptation of cellars under wine merchants' shops and public buildings. Church crypts were taken over as public shelters and tunnels in the cliffs to the east and west of the town were opened up and made bomb proof. Schools had basic shelters dug under the playgrounds. At **St Peters** some old chalk caves at Victoria Road were made safe and enlarged to take up to 250 individuals.

A huge number of people slept in these subterranean dug-outs each night. For instance, the 'Paragon' shelter on West Cliff at **Ramsgate** had room for 300 persons whilst the caves associated with The Grange were said to be capable of taking several thousand. Eventually all the shelters had electric lighting, seating and the entrances protected from blast with sandbags. They were all well organised and the Chief Constable of Ramsgate, S F Butler reported:

> "I am very pleased with the satisfactory manner in which the shelters are being worked. It relieves the police of a great responsibility. The caves at Hollicondane, the largest public dug-outs in the district, are also the best managed. An orderly crowd, almost entirely composed of women and children, is carefully mustered, and all the caves are thoroughly fumigated each morning. It is an exemplary practice."

In **Margate** the situation was similar with teams of volunteers modifying existing caves and tunnels and excavating new ones all over the town. A list of places where it was proposed to construct dug-outs, compiled in 1917, lists 29 sites including adapting Margate Caves, Clifton Baths, Margate Brewery Vaults and the digging of 26 new shelters. (See Appendix)

An opportunity to examine one of the volunteer constructed dug-outs occurred in 2007 when the rear lawn of a house in Northdown Park

Road, Cliftonville, subsided revealing what appeared to be the top a chalk tunnel at a depth of 3.4m below ground. The Kent Underground Research Group were called to investigate and, after some strenuous digging, gained access to a set of chalk tunnels.[11]

There were originally two public entrances from the road (now sealed) which led to a roughly circular passage. The tunnel leading up to the garden had, at some time, possibly during construction, a roof fall which blocked the way forward. This fall was by-passed by a new curving passage to skirt around the unstable part and the area of the fall sealed up.

The size of the passages of 1.65m high and only 0.7m wide is typical of many of the amateur constructed shelters.

The site of the shelter is mentioned on the list of proposed sites and is also shown on a map drawn up by Reeve and Bayly which shows all the public dug-outs and refuges used in the Great War (Information kindly supplied by Suzannah Foad of Margate Museum).

Graffiti cut into the chalk walls had the date range of 1917 to 1918 and included the names H. E. Cooper, J. Dyde and H. Bishop.

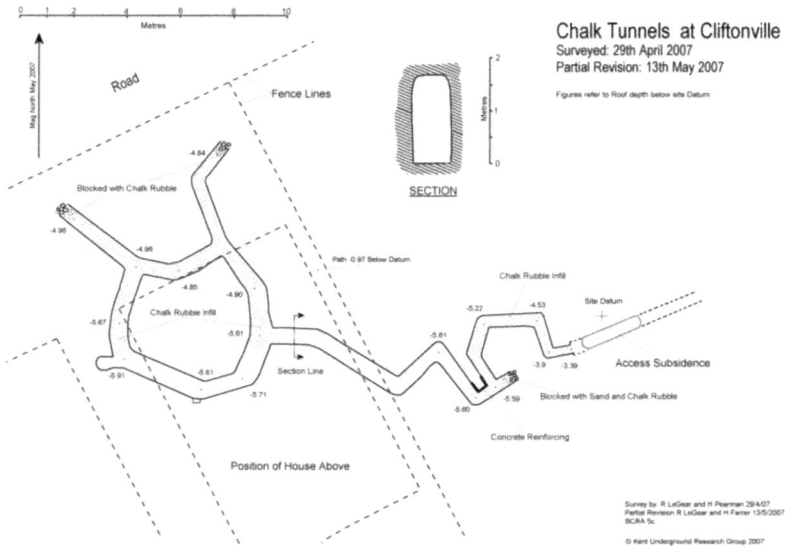

The tunnel from the garden was constructed to provide a private entrance to the refuge.

The house and garden was constructed in 1917 and was occupied by Ernest Brookes who was the Town Clerk of Margate at the time. His position in the community may have warranted his own private entrance.

© *KURG*

Another First World War shelter with a similar layout to Cliftonville example above was uncovered during the construction of an Asda store in Chatham Street, **Ramsgate** in January 2012 and surveyed by KURG shortly after.

Just inside the entrance was a well preserved wooden door frame set in concrete which sloped inward at the top, approx 15cm off vertical. This type of doorway was quite common in shelters and was designed to deflect blast. Any original steps leading down to the tunnel were covered with loose fill and debris. At the bottom of the steps the tunnel turned right to run approximately parallel with the surface boundary wall. This passage led to a roughly circular tunnel with a blocked entrance, also with a sloping door frame.

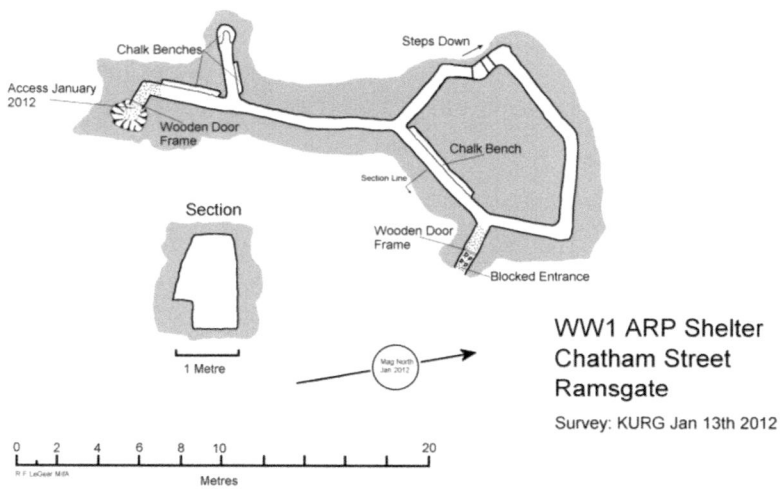

**WW1 ARP Shelter
Chatham Street
Ramsgate**
Survey: KURG Jan 13th 2012

The 50m of passages surveyed were of roughly rectangular cross section and between 1.7 and 1.9m high and 0.7 to 0.9m wide. This profile has been found to be fairly common in air-raid shelters dug during the First World War in Thanet.

© *Barry Stewart*

At four points in the system seating had been provided by means of benches cut into the side of the tunnels.

The many distinctive tool marks observed show that the tunnels had been excavated by means of a mechanical pick. The circular passage had been dug from two directions and a miscalculation caused a slight mis-alignment in both direction and height. The tunnel that was dug 'anti-clockwise' from the blocked entrance was 1.5m lower than the 'clockwise' one

 which resulted in a short joining link with three steps. The chalk steps showed little sign of wear which would suggest that the shelter was not heavily used. Lighting appeared to be by simple candles or oil lamps hanging from iron rods inserted in the walls. A number of candle niches were found, some still retaining short stubs of candle.

© *Pete Burton*

A great deal of graffiti in the form of pencil drawings was observed and a carved date of 1938. During that year many of the old First World War shelters and tunnels were examined to see if they would be suitable and/or safe for use as shelters in the coming conflict. There is no evidence that the tunnels were used in World War Two, perhaps because one entrance to the deep public shelter was nearby.

Ordnance Survey large scale plans covering the period of the First World War show the site as containing an Ice Factory. The shelter was almost certainly excavated in 1917 as a refuge for the staff and employees. The site was sealed and made safe shortly after the survey.

In May 2010 KURG were called to a development site off Ellington Place, **Ramsgate** by Andy Linklater of the Canterbury Archaeological Trust who had located a set of underground tunnels cut in the chalk.[12]

Ellington Girls School, which had originally been built in 1914 as Ellington School catering for 350 boys, 350 girls and 150 infants, had been demolished and the land cleared for housing development.

The tunnels, 2m high by 1.3m wide, had been used as an air-raid shelter in the Second World War by pupils and staff of the school whose buildings they ran under. The remains of bench seating were found in the two longest passages and some remains of electric lighting were visible.

Much graffiti from the 1940s was evident including a particularly fine drawing of the cartoon character 'Popeye'.

Three stairways led to the surface, all of which were sealed at the top with brick walls. Each department, i.e. Infants, Girls and Boys had their own entrance outside the school building. Two vertical shafts in the roof of the main passage were capped at the surface with concrete slabs and were probably construction shafts for the removal of spoil during excavation.

© *Barry Stewart*

Although the shelter was utilised in the 1939-45 conflict it is almost certain that it was dug in the First World War, as by 1917 all the schools in Ramsgate had been provided with shelters, most of which, like Ellington School, had lighting and bench seats.

At the end of the last war the cabling and light fittings were removed and the wooden seating from the benches was stripped out. Brick walls were constructed at the bottom of the initial fight of steps in each

© *KURG*

entrance and the stairways back-filled to the surface.

Unlike the Cliftonville shelter which had been dug utilising volunteer labour, the Ellington School and other school shelters which have been examined show they were dug in a much more professional way.

In 1917 the local council requested that soldiers should be used for the digging of additional shelters. It is probable that the Ellington shelter was constructed by men of the Northumberland Fusiliers, 100 of whom were allocated to Ramsgate for that purpose.

Similar First World War shelter tunnels have been recorded at Drapers Mill School and Clarendon House Grammar School, the latter having a World War Two shelter constructed above an earlier chalk tunnel shelter of World War One.

Shortly after the KURG investigation the Ellington tunnels were sealed and made safe so that the construction work could proceed.

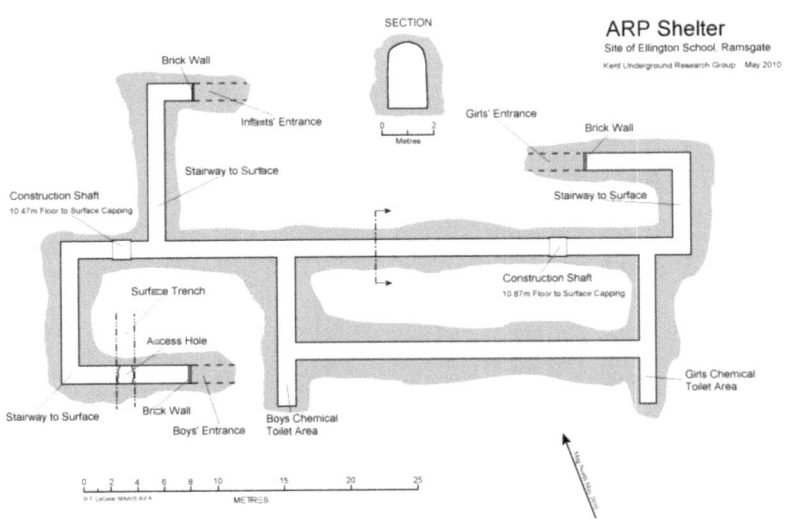

In the 1980s a set of chalk tunnels and a small room, probably of World War One date, were discovered during the excavation for a concrete pier at Addington Square, **Margate**. The tunnels were 2m high by 1m wide, originally accessed by two flights of chalk steps. These led to a small rectangular room with the remains of wooden benches at the sides. The tunnel continued to another entrance which was blocked with rubble. Small ledges had been cut at each corner to hold candles for illumination. It is understood that the tunnels were filled shortly after the brief examination by KURG member R. Whissen.

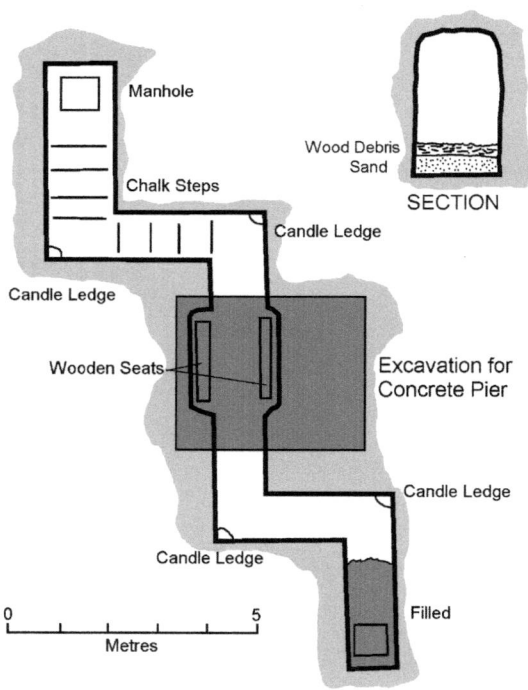

A simple private shelter was surveyed by KURG members Angie Runacre and Paul Wells in January 1994.[13]

A chalk passage had been discovered under a Victorian House in **Ramsgate** at NGR TR 3763 6481, and was entered via a short flight of chalk steps from the cellar. The main passage was found to be 1.9m high and 0.6m wide and had a recess along the western wall which formed a long bench. The passage then took a semi-circular route in a clockwise direction until it became blocked with rubble and earth. Beyond the infill it almost certainly originally exited in the garden as a secondary entrance.

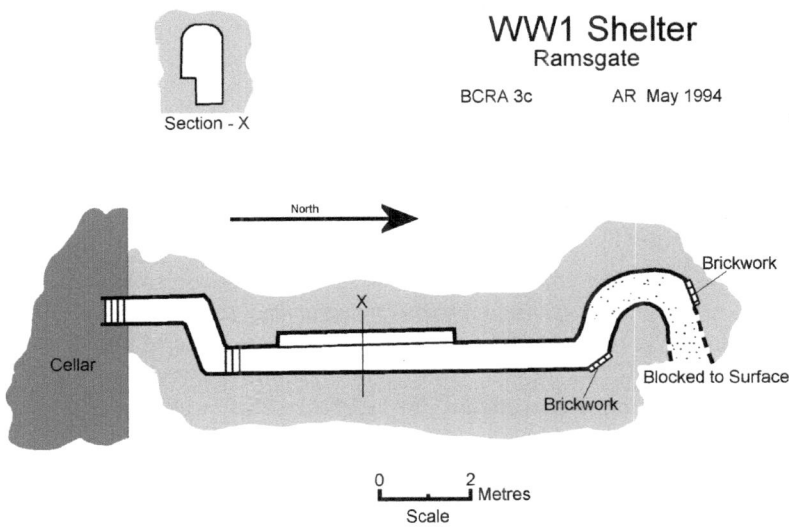

Some of the many tunnels and caves on the Island were employed by the armed services and adapted to military use. The tunnels associated with the many chalk pits in the vicinity of Manston Airfield were utilised as shelters in both world wars.

Those at Alland Grange and Cheeseman's Farm near **Manston** were adapted for shelter use and were much used by service personnel serving on the airfield as were the tunnels at Pouce's Farm and Vincent Farm.

The Alland Grange tunnels on the North West edge of the airfield were surveyed by a small team from the Kent Underground Research Group

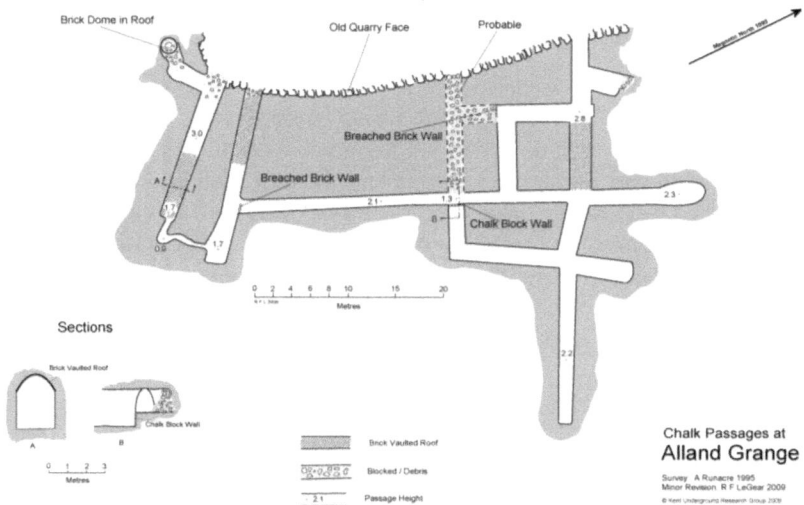

Chalk Passages at Alland Grange

led by Angie Runacre in 1995.¹⁴ A second visit was made in 2009 prior to the entrances being permanently sealed.¹⁵

At a time long after chalk extraction had ceased, the roofs of three of the galleries were strengthened by brick-lining the soffits. This probably occurred in World War One when the overlying road was taking heavy plant and traffic during the construction of an 'underground' hangar (see below) which was located a short distance away to the east.

The tunnels were used an air raid shelter from when Thanet came under aerial onslaught from enemy airships and Gotha bombers.

Between the wars in the 1930s the caves were used to grow mushrooms.

In the Second World War they were again used as a shelter for both the occupants of the Grange and nearby cottages as well as personnel from RAF Manston.

The underground hangars were created during the First World War when the airfield was a Royal Naval Air Station. Of the four originally planned, only two were completed by 1918, one near Alland Grange and the other to the north of the airfield alongside the Margate Road.

The hangars were not actually underground but were constructed below ground level with a wide sloping entrance ramp with the excavated chalk piled up on the three other sides of the pit. It is not thought that the hangars were ever properly roofed; rather they would have had camouflage netting stretched over the top. Small caves were excavated in the sides of the pits for use as workshops and stores etc.

The station historian and author of 'The History of RAF Manston' (3rd edition 1986) Flt Lt R Stockman MAIE RAF writes:

> *"I suspect that the hangars were used as large working areas for the groundcrews and to provide protection from high winds and, more importantly, bomb and shell blasts."*

The Margate Road site was filled in over a number of years but the Alland Grange one still exists and is now occupied by an equestrian centre.

Ramsgate's Deep ARP Shelters

In 1938, with another war on the horizon, Ramsgate Council embarked on an ambitious plan to provide deep underground protection for its citizens which was to result in one of the largest public shelters in the country. This was quite radical at the time as the Government were against the idea of providing deep shelters as they wrongly assumed that the population would hide in shelters all day leaving no one to run the industry and war effort of the country.

The system was devised by the Borough Engineer, R D Brimmell, and vigorously promoted by Ramsgate's flamboyant Mayor, A B C Kempe. In 1939 the go-ahead was given by the government and initially a disused 1,650yard (1.5km) railway tunnel, together with a spur tunnel used by a scenic railway, was adapted for shelter use. Deep tunnels were then excavated running around the town from the western harbour in a semi-circle to the railway tunnel in the east. The contractor, Cementation Ltd, dug the 3.25miles (5.3km) of new tunnels under the roads and streets of the town at depths of up to 70ft (20m) below ground. The work went on 24 hours a day much to the annoyance of some residents who complained about the constant noise. Virtually the whole system was dug under council owned or controlled land so there were no problems of access. The thousands of tonnes of chalk excavated from the tunnels were dumped on the western foreshore between the West Pier and the Undercliff Promenade to form the foundation for a planned new section of promenade which was never constructed.

© *Barry Stewart*

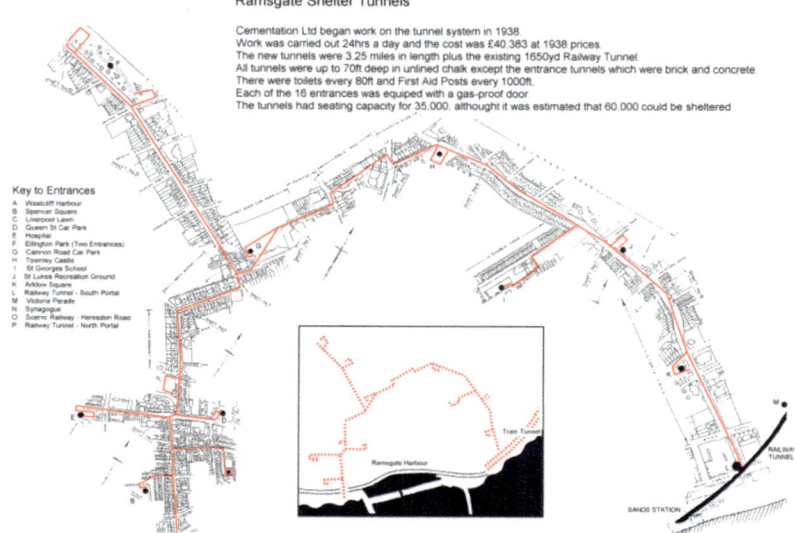

Ramsgate Shelter Tunnels

Cementation Ltd began work on the tunnel system in 1938.
Work was carried out 24hrs a day and the cost was £40,383 at 1938 prices.
The new tunnels were 3.25 miles in length plus the existing 1650yd Railway Tunnel.
All tunnels were up to 70ft deep in unlined chalk except the entrance tunnels which were brick and concrete.
There were toilets every 80ft and First Aid Posts every 1000ft.
Each of the 16 entrances was equiped with a gas-proof door.
The tunnels had seating capacity for 35,000, althought it was estimated that 60,000 could be sheltered.

Key to Entrances
A Westcliff Harbour
B Spencer Square
C Liverpool Lawn
D Queen St Car Park
E Hospital
F Ellington Park (Two Entrances)
G Cannon Road Car Park
H Townley Castle
I St Georges School
J St Lukes Recreation Ground
K Arklow Square
L Railway Tunnel - South Portal
M Victoria Parade
N Synagogue
O Scenic Railway - Hereseaton Road
P Railway Tunnel - North Portal

© *Nick Catford*

The main tunnels were 7ft (2.1m) high by 6ft (1.8m) wide through unlined chalk with chemical toilets in recesses every 80ft (24.3m) and First Aid posts every 1000ft. (304m) An entrance was specially constructed to connect Ramsgate Hospital with the shelter system to allow patients access and also to be used for getting casualties to the hospital from other parts of the town if the roads had become blocked and impassable.

All of the 16 entrances around the town had steel gas proof doors and the entrance tunnels were lined with 12in (30.5cm) of reinforced concrete. The entrance stairways were 10ft (3.0m) wide and concrete lined near the surface. The hospital entrance did not use steps but a sloping passage for easier transportation of patients.

There was seating for 35,000 people although it was estimated that 60,000 could be accommodated in extreme conditions.

The shelter was equipped with electric lighting from the town's main supply although the Queen Street section had its own batteries and generator.

© *Kent Photo Archive – War and Peace Collection*

After the mains power failed one night the council bought 200 hurricane lamps as an emergency light source.

This vast underground tunnel system, together with the various other shelters around the town provided a number of shelter spaces that exceeded the population of the town. This made Ramsgate the best town in the country for providing safe refuge for its citizens. In 1944 there were plans to use at least some of the tunnel system for storage as a letter from the Ministry of Supply to the Home office dated 14th November 1944 stated:

> "....Ramsgate would be very useful for our purpose and requested their transfer ASAP to Min of Supply for Min of Supply storage."

This would probably have been for emergency stocks of food although there is no evidence that any of the tunnels were ever handed over to the Ministry.

During the Cold War in 1951 the forward thinking Borough Engineer produced a plan to re-use the World War Two tunnels as nuclear shelters. The Ellington Road section was to be widened to by-pass a sewer that had been laid in the tunnel after the war. He also drew up plans for extending the system by digging a new 700 yard (640m) tunnel under London Road to the east of the town and another 1.62 miles (2.6km) long to serve the Newington area to the north. This would have given a total of over 4 miles (6.4km) of deep shelter tunnels to serve 41,000 people. In 1954 the Ministry of Works inspected the war time tunnels with a view to the Home Office reserving them for air raid shelters. The proposed extensions to the system were never dug as thankfully the much feared nuclear war did not materialise. The existing tunnels were then abandoned and largely forgotten.

Over the last few years there has been a campaign to have at least part of the tunnels open to the public and in 2011 the Ramsgate Tunnels Heritage Group applied for Lottery funding via the Jubilee People's Millions and thanks to the support of local residents the project was awarded a £50,000 grant. The funds are to be used to research and record the design, construction and history of the tunnels and to carry out surveys with a view to re-opening them as an all weather heritage attraction and venue. For up to date news of the project see the web site: www.ramsgatetunnels.org.

Tunnel historian, Phil Spain, has produced the results of his painstaking research into the tunnels in a book which charts the evolution of Ramsgate's shelter history. The title: *Ramsgate Has the World's Finest Shelters* was taken from a quote in the War Illustrated Magazine for September 1940 (See Further Study).

In addition to the public shelters many firms and companies provided their own refuges for their employees by adapting existing vaults and cellars and also constructing new underground shelters.

One such example was at the **Rank Flour Mills at Ramsgate** where, on the eve of war, two new shelters were dug: one for the men under the old railway cattle pens to the rear of the site and one for the office staff under the mill itself.

In 2005 the site was sold by Rank Hovis to a developer who kindly allowed an examination of the office shelter tunnels in January 2007.[16]

A brick lined passage led from beneath the general office to an 'L' shaped tunnel, one section of which was of larger dimensions to allow its use as an underground office during raids. A second way out was provided which exited via another set of stairs onto Margate Road.

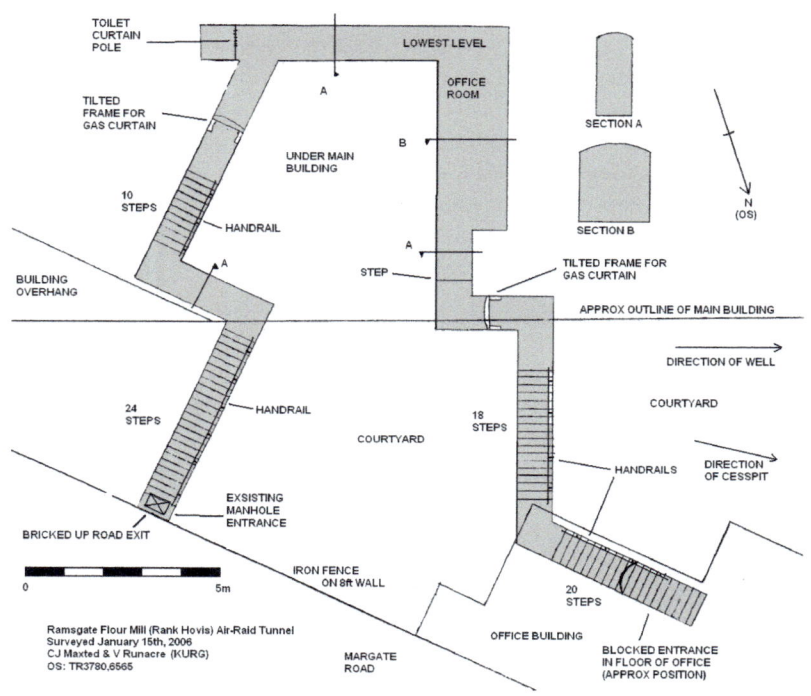

© *Vince Runacre*

Two heavy curtains were installed as an anti-gas precaution and an alcove was provided to house a chemical toilet (the ubiquitous 'Elsan').

When the warning of an impending attack was sounded office workers were expected to pick up their files and ledgers and descend into the shelter where they would carry on work until the all clear siren was heard.

The construction of the two shelters was a wise move by the Mill owners as the site was hit by nine bombs during raids, including one which did not explode.

During the Second World War Thanet's fighter station, **RAF Manston** was a prime target for enemy bombers. The German plan in the early years of the war was to destroy the airfields of the Royal Air Force to gain air superiority prior to launching an invasion. As one of the closest airfields to the Channel, Manston was subjected to many severe raids.

Several existing chalk caves were used as refuges from the heavy air raids and many new underground shelters were constructed around the airfield. After the war these shelters were backfilled and in many cases their exact locations were lost.

One shelter was discovered on October 1st 2004 when contractors preparing the ground for a new car park south of the terminal building at Kent International Airport broke through the roof of a chalk passage. Wooden roof props and some corrugated iron sheets were visible from the surface some 4m above.

The Kent Underground Research Group was asked to carry out an investigation which was undertaken on October 3rd 2004.[17]

The shelter consisted of a single main passage 1.3m wide with an estimated height of 1.8 to 2m. The lowest attainable point was found to be 6.25m from the surface to the top of the chalk and corrugated iron debris that completely covered the original floor.

The passage had the remains of 5in x 4in (127mm x 104mm) wooden props spaced at 15in (38cm) intervals supporting cross beams of similar dimensions.

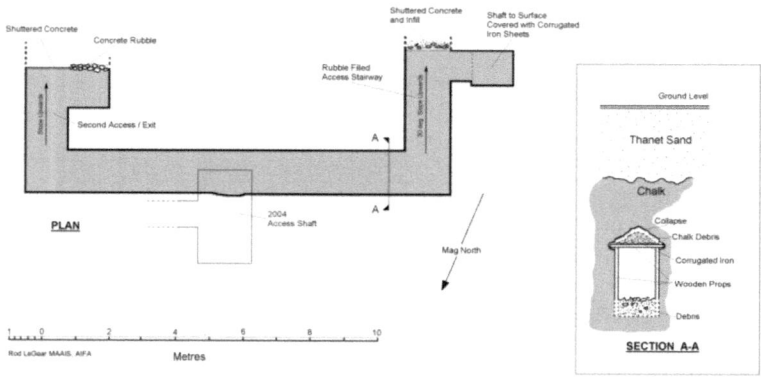

Underground Shelter
Kent International Airport, Manston

The ends of the cross beams had been inserted into specially cut holes in the chalk walls and fastened in place by jamming bricks between the wood and the chalk. A number of these bricks were still in situ, although in many cases the timber had rotted away. Corrugated iron sheets had been laid over the cross beams to provide a roof safe from minor chalk falls.

The few remaining supports were found to be in a perilous condition; most had collapsed allowing the corrugated iron roof to collapse. At least one of the props had been re-used from a surface building as half its surface was covered in green paint. The treated wood had survived in much better condition than the other timber in the shelter. This second-hand use of materials could indicate that the shelter was dug in something of a hurry using whatever timber (probably from a bomb damaged building) that was easily available.

From a small intact section of the passage, it could be seen that since the shelter's construction the original chalk roof had been slowly flaking away, thus forming a void above a growing pile of chalk rubble lying on the corrugated iron. When the roof collapsed this chalk rubble added to the general debris covering the floor.

The pattern of the fallen chalk and corrugated iron indicated that the total failure occurred when the roof was breached by the contractor's mechanical excavator.

The original access to the structure was via two sloping tunnels leading up from each end of, and at 90 degrees to, the main passage. As in the main passage the original floors of these tunnels could not be reached, but it is probable that under the chalk debris were the remains of stairways. Both of these tunnels were found to have been deliberately blocked by shuttered concrete walls and infill. It is likely that the access tunnels would have turned through a further right angle shortly after the blockage as an anti-blast precaution. At the side of what appeared to be the main entrance was found a roughly square vertical shaft (1.1m x 1.37m) leading up towards the surface but sealed by corrugated iron sheets roughly at the junction of the Chalk and Thanet Sand. This was probably a ventilation shaft although it could also have been used as emergency exit. Subsequent excavations by the contractors located a concrete slab 1.0m below the surface at this position.

No discernable graffiti could be found and the only artefacts discovered were two rusting runway edge light housings and a milk bottle from the dairy 'Pace' which may indicate that the shelter's entrances were used to dump rubbish before being sealed permanently.

An aerial photo of RAF Manston taken from 11,000ft on 11th Jan. 1939 gives no indication of shelter entrances at that point, although at this time the need for a generous number of deep shelters was not fully appreciated. A later aerial photo from 1940 shows the aftermath of a heavy bombing raid by the Luftwaffe with several High Explosive bomb craters across the field and admin areas.

It is most likely that the shelter described above was dug at this time when Manston was rapidly becoming the most heavily attacked fighter station in the country. There are probably many such shelters around the airfield, their presence and location unknown at this time.

An interesting set of tunnels was revealed in February 2001 when part of the front garden of a house in the High Street, **St Peters** suddenly collapsed.

The subsidence had been caused by the failure of the roof of a chalk tunnel lying approx. 4.2m below the surface. The soak-away for the house had concentrated water over a point above the void, and over a period of almost thirty years, had weakened the chalk until a catastrophic collapse occurred.

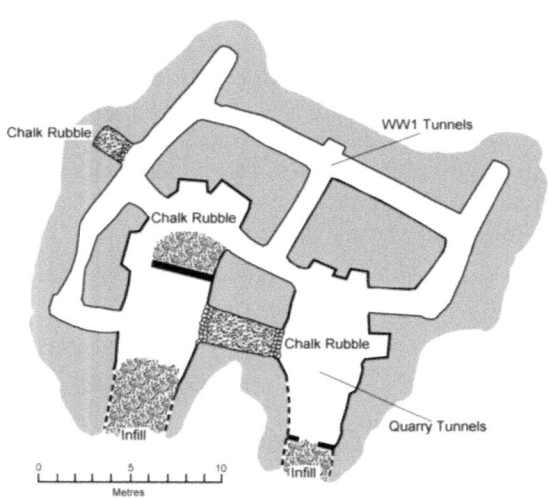

A survey by the Kent Underground Research Group found that a large cone of debris over 3m high obscured the floor of the tunnel which was estimated to have been originally 3m high and 3 to 4m wide at that point. To the west, under the garden of the neighbouring house, the tunnel was blocked by infill from behind a wooden doorway of later construction. A similar sized passage was found to the north with a series of smaller passages connecting the two. That tunnel was also blocked to the west; this time by a large amount of cement grouting that had been poured in from the surface and had solidified in a steep cone. A brick and flint wall had been built in this passage up to roof height but was not load bearing.

Three rectangular holes, similar to military firing loopholes had been incorporated near the top of the construction. A large pile of chalk rubble was found piled in the angle between the brick wall and the natural chalk wall. A cross-gallery joining the two larger tunnels had been filled with similar chalk rubble and the two ends sealed with retaining walls of chalk blocks from floor to roof. Another short blind adit in the smaller tunnels was also backfilled and sealed in this way.

At some time after the excavation of the main tunnels had ceased the eastern ends were enlarged and a number of alcoves were cut into the walls and carefully numbered in black painted numerals. If these bays were designed to be used as storage areas there is no evidence that they were ever used as such.

The smaller passages were on average 2m high by 1.5m wide with the roof level being approx. 4.1m below the surface. A number of wooden candleholders were still in-situ at various points. Tool marks from the miner's picks were in abundance in these adits and it was possible to determine the direction of excavation. Some of the passages had been dug from opposing directions and the slight miss-alignment when they met was apparent in a couple of areas.

The tunnels do not appear to have suffered from any significant roof falls except for the major collapse that exposed the site.

In the 18th century a small open quarry (approx 30m west of the subsidence site) was extracting chalk for lime burning and/or agricultural use. Two tunnels were driven from the pit and connected underground by at least one cross passage. A date of 1784 carved in the wall confirms the dating.

The 'storage' areas and the smaller tunnels were dug later – dates from the First World War are numerous with names and service numbers of military personnel. The excavated chalk from these later tunnels was not taken out of the workings, but used to fill the earlier cross passage and one of the newer blind headings. Some of the unwanted chalk was left in a heap by the brick wall, which had been constructed about the same time. When chalk is mined or quarried all of the material is useful so backfilling a tunnel is most unproductive. The many candleholders show that lighting was by means of an open flame, which would indicate that the tunnels were unlikely to have been dug to provide storage for ammunition or explosives.

Further dates and names on the walls show that the site was accessible by individuals and whole families up until the late 1930's. By the Second World War the army was again interested in the site and a few dates, names and ranks of 1942 and 43 were found. It is possible the tunnels were being checked for suitability at that time for some military purpose. There is no evidence that they were used for such, or that they were used as air raid shelters. Simple chalk extraction was clearly not the reason for the digging of the later tunnels.

One possibility is that the army dug the newer excavations as practice tunnels for training sappers before sending them to France in the First World War. This could explain the walling up of the chalk rubble. During the First World War many kilometres of tunnels and dugouts were excavated for communication and shelter. Heaps of pure white chalk being removed would give the enemy the position of a tunnel entrance and invite heavy shelling. It was therefore sometimes prudent to backfill older tunnels that had become unsafe or no longer used to conceal some of the spoil. The brick wall could have been a model of an underground defence position. Such positions were constructed in case the enemy gained access to the tunnel system. Similar training tunnels have been recorded in the county and it is probable that many more await discovery.

The old pit from which the larger tunnels were dug is now part of a private garden and the tunnel entrances have been long buried under falls from the old quarry face.

In late 1940 a network of underground battle headquarters was established by South East Army Command with tunnels systems excavated at Tunbridge Wells, Canterbury and Reigate. These centres would have directed the troops fighting the enemy forces had a successful invasion taken place

There was also an underground Brigade HQ located in a disused quarry at **Sarre** which reported to the Battle HQ at Canterbury. The following description is based on information from the Subterranea Britannica web site of the survey in 1998 by Andy Miles and Paul Wells when access was still possible.

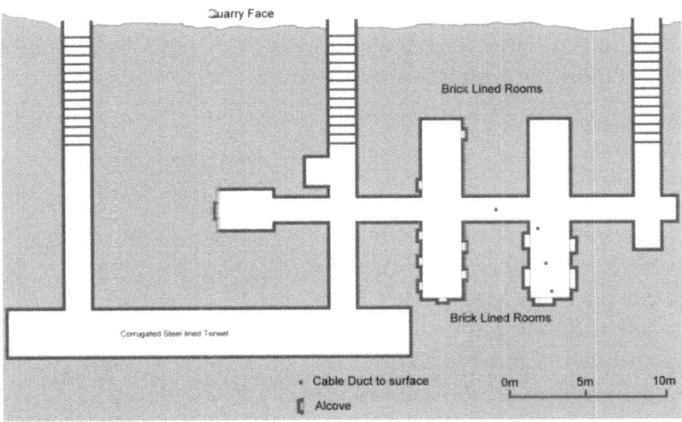

After Subterranea Britannica

The brigade headquarters consisted of three parallel stairways cut into the northern face of an old chalk quarry. These descended 50ft (15.2m) into a small series of tunnels and rooms.

Two of the stairways led directly into a main corridor which was brick lined for most of its length but the western end was unlined in chalk with the remains of rotting timber pit props; this section appeared to be unfinished. There were two brick lined rooms on either side of the corridor with a third room at the eastern end. Two of these rooms still retained lettering on the brick work; one labelled 'Sigs' indicating that it was a signals room and the other labelled 'Clerks Int Sec'. Three metal pipes used as cable ducts protruded from the roof of one room which originally carried cables to the surface. A fourth cable duct was located in the ceiling of the corridor.

The third stairway led to a 35m long tunnel supported with steel hoops and lined with corrugated steel sheets, similar to the many coastal battery deep shelters found along the Kent Coast.

The floor was littered with rubble from minor roof falls but the brick lined sections of the tunnels were generally in good condition although timber door frames were found to be rotting or have gone altogether.

After the war, the three entrances were bricked up but when visited in 1998 access to the eastern stairway was possible as the corrugated steel lining that protruded some distance out from the quarry face had largely rotted away. The other two stairways had been backfilled with rubble.

Since that date the three entrance tunnels have been bulldozed and all evidence of their position has now been lost.

HMS Fervent

Under the East Cliff below Wellington Crescent, Ramsgate are a series of chalk cut caves which may have been originally dug by local fishermen for storage purposes. A long tunnel links them together and continues up to the cliff top and would have been used for gaining easy access to the beach below. It was almost certainly used by 'free traders' as a way of getting landed contraband goods covertly up the cliff.

In the Great War the tunnels were used as basic shelters and in the Second World War they were utilised as part of a military base.

© Barry Stewart

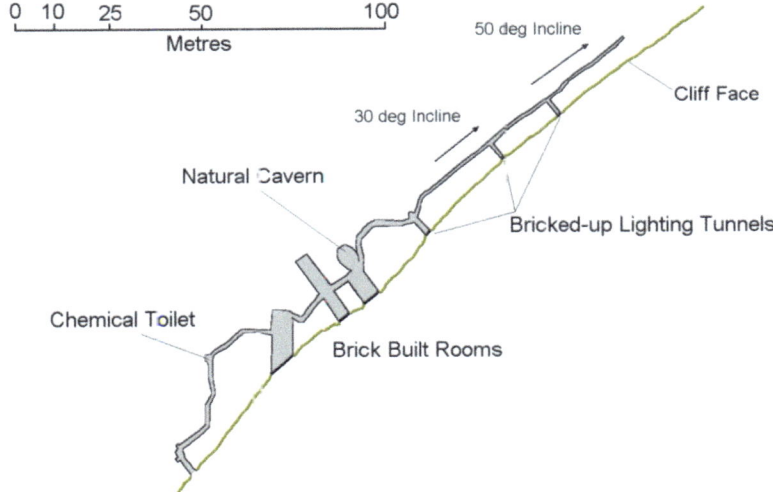

In October 1939 a Royal Navy shore station was commissioned to the east of the harbour. This station, known as HMS Fervent, took over the 'Merrie England' amusement park buildings to use as accommodation for naval ratings and new huts were erected for the administration staff.

The tunnels behind the site under East Cliff were taken over and used as an ARP shelter and as the base ammunition magazine. Brick walls and rooms were constructed in the three large caves, one of which was used as a communications centre. From 1941 Fervent was used as a Coastal Forces base

© *Barry Stewart*

with Motor Torpedo Boats (MTB) and Motor Gun Boats (MGB) keeping the coastal waters free of enemy shipping.. The site was relinquished by the Navy at the end of hostilities in 1945.[18]

Home Guard Auxiliary Units

In the Second World War a top secret resistance force was formed in order to fight a guerrilla war had the Germans invaded. Although technically part of the Home Guard, the regular Home Guard members had no idea of its existence. The Auxiliary Units as they were known were made up of men who had an excellent knowledge of their local area such as farmers, foresters, gamekeepers and poachers.

Each of the unit patrols had their own underground Operational Base (OB) which was large enough to hold seven men. The OB would have bunks, a cooking stove together with food and water for several weeks. They were all very well hidden and often had ingeniously built entrances. Smaller underground observation posts were also dug to allow secret surveillance of enemy troop movements.

The Thanet group, commanded by local farmer Norman Steed, turned several of the old existing tunnels on the island into suitable hideouts.

Whilst looking for suitable sites he discovered an old chalk tunnel at the edge of Manston airfield leading under the runways. He explored it with his intelligence officer and found it blocked by a roof fall about 150ft (45.7m) in. Plans were made to send in a team of sappers to clear out the obstruction but before that could occur the airfield was bombed and the tunnel blocked permanently.

The Manston patrol then had a hideout constructed by the Royal Engineers in the side of an old pit at a brickworks near Lydden, north of Manston.

A horizontal tunnel was dug from the side of the pit and a 14ft by 8ft (4.3m x 2.4m) chamber made. A shaft to the surface was excavated, emerging under a machine shop. The entrance tunnel was constructed in a false wooden retaining wall under a pile of ash. By pressing a bent nail a section of the planking would swing inward giving access to the tunnel.Requiring a second Operational Base they made another hideout in the old cellar of the original farmhouse at Nash Court which had burnt down some time before.

In David Lampe's book 'The Last Ditch' (p102) the author notes:

"At Manston, not far from Margate, an auxiliary unit patrol decided to put its hideout in a man-made cave, believed to have been scooped out of the chalk in the 17th century by members of a religious order. To make sure their hideout would not be discovered by the Germans, the Welsh tunnellers who made it went to the trouble of excavating a new branch off one of the old passages. They concealed the room with a huge block of chalk that they mounted on rollers"

(See also Nash Court Cave below).

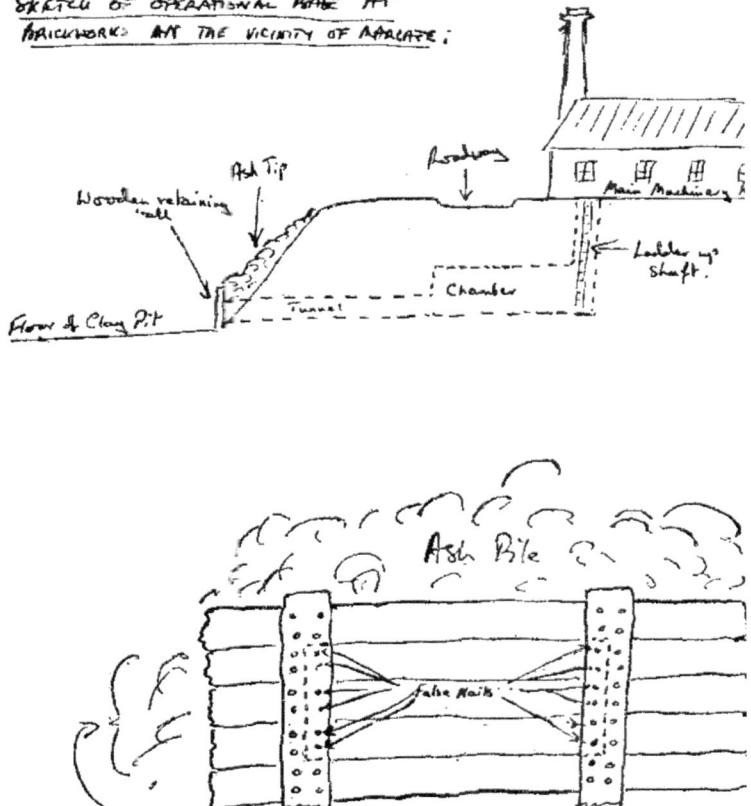

Sketch by Colonel Field

Transport

Many tunnels were constructed simply to convey people from one place to another, commonly from the top of a cliff to the bottom. Undoubtedly some of these were dug or utilised by members of smuggling gangs bringing consignments of contraband goods landed on the beach up to the land above.

A number of large houses and hotels also had tunnels and passages cut in order to have a convenient and private access to the beach.

Perhaps the most famous example of a beach access is the set of stairs cut inside the cliffs at **North Foreland**. In 1914 the author John Buchan was staying at Broadstairs when his small daughter was recovering from an operation. In the garden of a villa called St Cuby was a set of tunnelled stairways leading down to the beach which it is said inspired him to write his famous best selling novel 'The 39 Steps'.

The stairs consist of two shafts and three tunnelled sections and at the time of Buchan's stay there were actually 78 oak steps which he reduced with artistic licence to 39 in the book as a more suitable number. In the 1940s the wooden steps were replaced with 108 concrete ones. Book ends were made from some pieces of the replaced woodwork and were presented to the owners of St Cuby and to Alfred Hitchcock who produced the film of the book. The concrete steps are currently crumbling away and access is now prohibited.

The villa has been converted to luxury self catering apartments but the top entrance to the stairs can still be seen surrounded by bushes as in the book. There are at least two other similar tunnelled staircases in the area which have been fully sealed up.[19]

Some of these beach access tunnels were quite elaborate with extra tunnels and rooms dug to form small grottos. One such site was surveyed by KURG members in February 1992 which led from the former Wishing Towers Hotel on the Eastern Esplanade at **Cliftonville**.[20]

In 1991 when the hotel was being converted to a residential home a tunnel was discovered behind a bricked up entrance in the cellar. Two flights of steep worn steps led down to a narrow, varying between 0.45m and 1.46m wide, 2m high tunnel cut in the chalk which continued north towards Cliftonville Beach until it was blocked by a roof fall.

A bricked up entrance to a similar sized tunnel can be seen about 3m up the cliff face, just above the high water level, on the projected line of the tunnel. The investigators noted that there was evidence that at one time the stairway had a handrail to assist

© *Angie Runacre*

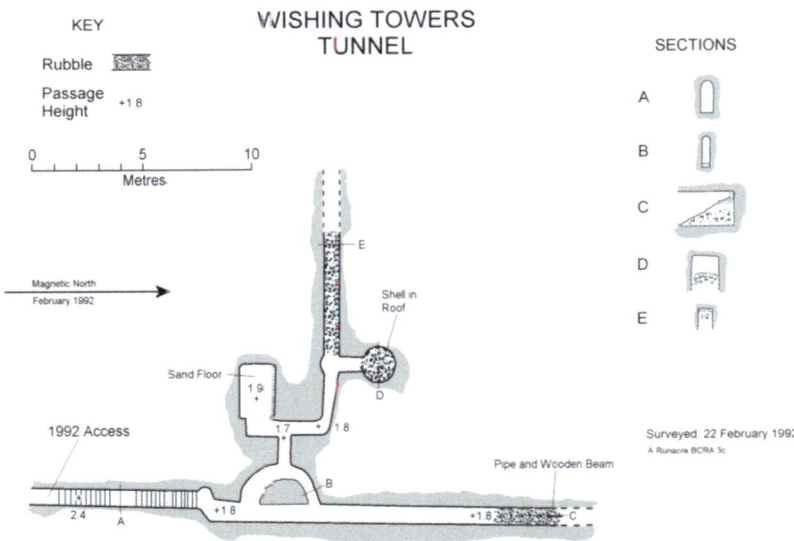

with the steep descent. A little way along the passage from the bottom of the stairs another set of passages led off to the west. In a rubble filled circular chamber in this area, the owner of the hotel found a Victorian bucket and spade and two glass drinks siphons.

The western passage is also blocked with rubble and spoil, probably from a roof fall.

The hotel building appears to have been built in the mid 1920s and it is probable that the tunnels were dug shortly after.

In 1843 Augustus Pugin, the well known architect and designer of the interior of the Houses of Parliament, bought an acre of land facing the sea at **Ramsgate** and built 'The Grange' which continued to be occupied by the Pugin family until 1928.

Pugin had an underground route to the sea front, where he had a mooring for a boat that he owned called 'The Caroline'. A tunnel led from the house to the cliff, and within the cliff was dug an underground 'ball room' with galleried windows looking out over the sea, it was also known as the 'Blue Room' on account of the colour of its tiling. A whole series of tunnels under the seaward end of the property were interconnected, some of which almost certainly pre-dated the Grange and Pugin's excavations.

An undated estate agent's note states:

> *"THE CAVES comprise numerous underground Galleries, flights of steps and Chambers carried under the Promenade to the face of the cliff and approached from the Entrance Hall of the House and also by a flight of steps at the bottom of the Garden. About halfway down the cliff lead to two sheltered TERRACES in the face of the cliff, having beds planted with fig trees; ROOM with brick-arched roof, tiled floor with fish pond and windows overlooking sea, ROOM with bricked arched roof and windows overlooking the sea.*
>
> *Lower down and on a level with the Western Undercliff Promenade, the galleries lead to long cemented TERRACE with iron railing; two smaller TERRACES; ROOM with glazed front; small TERRACE with W.C., and a long, cemented TERRACE having iron railing, timber erection of Shop with glazed front and side. Electric light is laid into the Rooms, Shop and some of the galleries and chambers".*

In World War One the tunnels were used as an air-raid shelter and were said to be capable of holding several thousand. In the 1930s they were opened to the public as the 'Smugglers Caves' using the entrance at the bottom of the Grange garden. In World War Two it was decided to adapt the underground features once again to make a public shelter and an entrance was created beyond the garden wall by the path called Screaming Alley. In 1944 the vibrations from nearby heavy guns triggered a severe collapse which damaged the cliff top. In 1947 another collapse caused the brick piers supporting the road to fail and a large section of the cliff fell away destroying most of the tunnel complex.

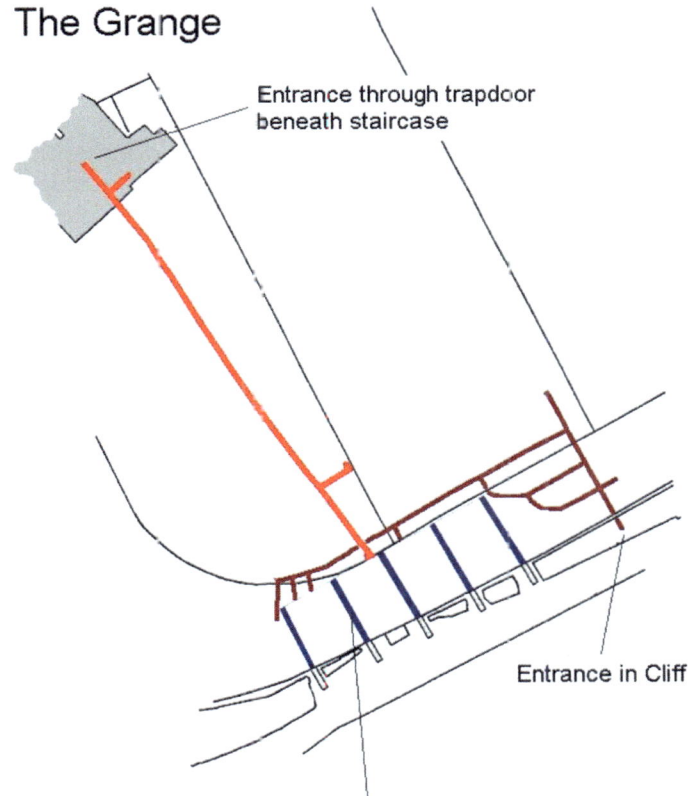

In 2002 KURG were approached by Donald Insoll, an architectural company who were working with the Landmark Trust on refurbishing the Grange, to survey the surviving underground features.

© *KURG*

The tunnel from the house was found to be still intact but now sealed at the coast end with concrete blocks. A small section of tunnel over 150m in length under the road was also surveyed which, before the wartime collapse, would have joined with the passage from the house and other lower level tunnels. A record was made of the graffiti within the passages with the earliest being noted as the date of 1867 carved into a stone block on the floor. There were a number of dates in the 1930s and 1940s and a sizeable number from 1988.[21]

To the east of **Ramsgate** on the Eastcliff, beneath King George VI Park, there is another extensive network of chalk passages, known as the **Granville Caves** or **Eastcliff Caverns**. As with Pugin's tunnels the Granville Caves were also used as public shelters during both world wars. Access is not now possible but a good description from a Victorian newspaper states:

> *"The caverns at East Cliff deserve particular notice: they are formed by an excavation at the distance of thirty feet from the cliff, and parallel with it, descending gradually to the level of the shore. This subterraneous passage receives its light from arches of such large capacity as to resemble rooms, which are cut at right angles through the chalky cliffs opening to the sea and these arches being in summer carpeted with turf, and covered with shrubs and flowers, appear very picturesque. The lowest arch terminates in a passage leading directly to the beach."*

From the Eastern undercliff, you can still clearly see blocked up entrances to these tunnels in the cliff face. Higher up in the cliff, some of these entrances still remain open although inaccessable. They appear to be still carpeted with turf, as described in the old account above, over a hundred years ago.[22]

© *Vince Runacre*

Enigmatic Sites

The outline of a small cave was exposed in the south-west corner of a chalk quarry at Spratling Court Farm, **Manston** in 1996. The site was investigated by Colin A Baker of St Lawrence College, Ramsgate between 1996 and 2007 and a comprehensive report was produced.[23]

The cave was full of natural infill and had a vertical shaft like entrance and a short low horizontal passage. Tool marks from an iron pick were noted but no dateable artefacts were found during the examination. Radio Carbon dating of animal bones found in the infill together with the presence of a particular species of snail gave an early to mid Roman date.

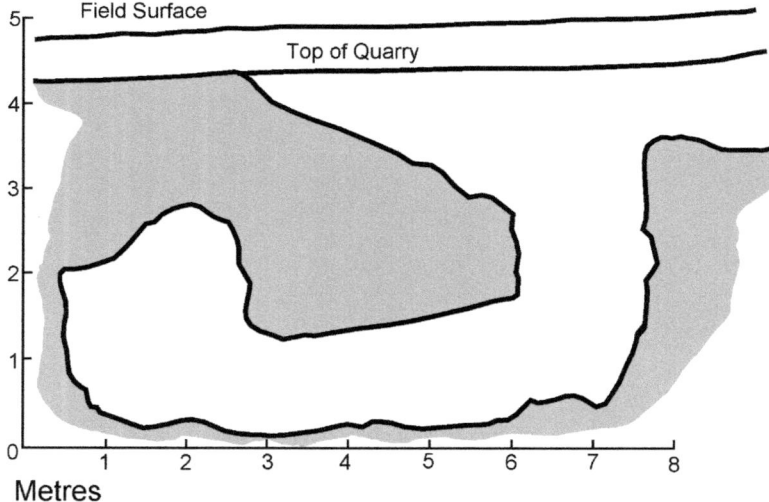

Although it was not possible to give a definitive reason for its excavation it was thought that it may have been a ritual shaft. A somewhat similar, although smaller, ritual feature was examined by Keith Parfitt at Mill Hill, Deal in 1984.[24]

Underground Chapel, St Nicholas at Wade

The structure under part of the garden of St Nicholas Court, St Nicholas at Wade, has been described as either an underground chapel or a crypt. It certainly has an ecclesiastical feel about it and consists of a cruciform shaped room entered by a relatively modern tunnel and flight of steps from a wing of the Court. It is built of chalk block walls with a barrel vaulted roof also of carefully cut chalk blocks. There are a number of elaborate niches constructed in the walls presumably for some significant purpose.

At some time in the past the roof of the north-west arm of the cross collapsed, probably blocking the original entrance passage. This section was walled off and the present entrance constructed, possibly in the 19th century.

© Paul Wells

A detailed assessment of the chapel/crypt was made by P. J. C. Lambert and K. H. McIntosh and the result of their research was published in the Kent Archaeological Society journal Archaeologia Cantiana.[25] This paper expanded and added to the unpublished notes of the late Ken Gravett, an acknowledged authority on building recording, who had visited the site on a number of occasions before his untimely death in 1998. He believed that the style of construction was that of the 14th century.

© Paul Wells

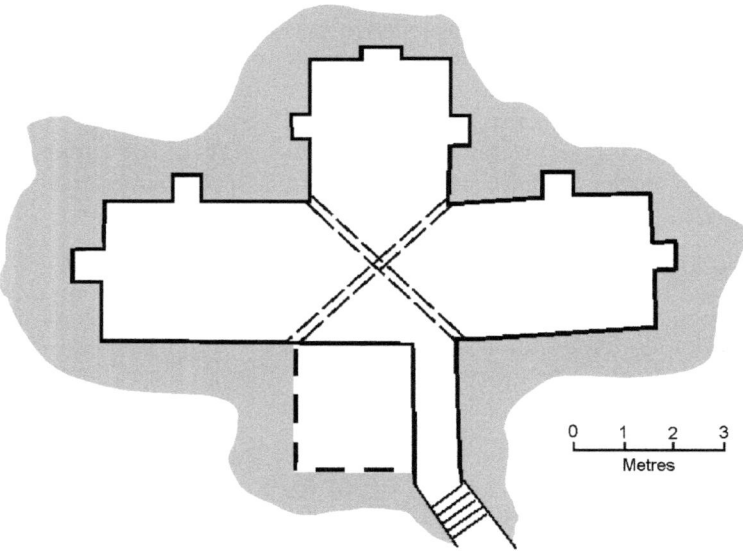

St Nicholas Court Underground Chapel

Current thinking suggests that, although the original use cannot be proved definitively, it is likely that the site was a crypt beneath a ground level chapel or a chapel beneath a house. Another theory is that this was constructed as secret religious meeting place.

Nash Court Cave

A site with many similarities with the St Nicholas at Wade underground chapel once existed at Nash Court near **Manston**.

In 1878 the Rev. W. A. Scott wrote some notes on Thanet in volume XXII. (1878) of Archaeologia Cantiana.

He commented that in the garden behind Nash Court was a series of chambers excavated in the chalk and that an inscribed stone in a nearby wall stated that in 1782:

"The entrance was arched over and covered with earth"

The chambers were cruciform in plan and it was thought that the original entrance was via a circular stairway at the end of one of the arms of the cross. At the time of the Rev. Scott's comments the access was by a flight of steps which took up the whole of one chamber.

The chambers were described as being vaulted in chalk of Norman character and having arched niches in the walls. Scott thought that the excavation may have been made as early as the 15th century or as late as the 17th. Suggestions as to its original function ranged from a secret oratory to a hidden cellar used by smugglers. The Ward Locke and Co. guide to Margate for 1905 described the site and suggested that it was used: *"as a secret chapel in the days of religious persecution"*.

In 1958 S. G. A. Luff cleared the debris from the entrance with help from some pupils of Abbey School. A few years later he returned to the site with Subterranea Britannica member Derek Fuller who photographed the structure and took some measurements.

© *Derek Fuller*

The photographs show that, like the St Nicholas site, it was constructed of chalk blocks with carefully constructed vaulted roofs.[26]

On this visit it was found that the 18th century brickwork arch had collapsed onto the entrance steps. Inside a wall had apparently fallen in to reveal a tunnel which led towards a nearby cellar.

Fuller concluded that this was a World War Two addition to utilise the site as an air raid shelter.

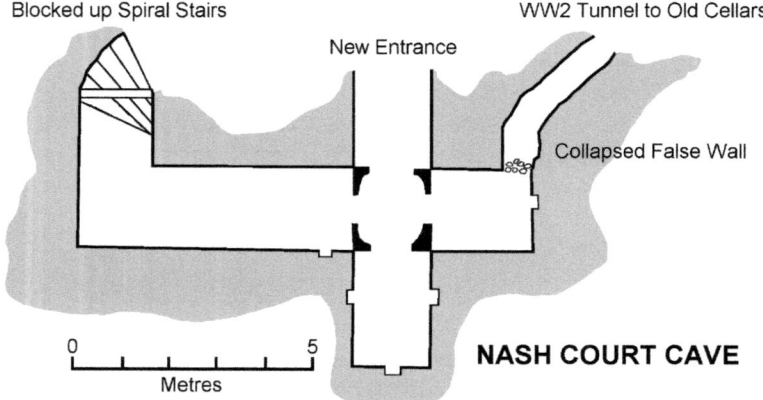

Further research has shown that this tunnel was indeed from the Second World War but was not dug as part of a shelter but as a Home Guard Auxiliary Unit's Operational Base. (See above).

The collapsed wall noted by Fuller was almost certainly rubble from the failure of the chalk block hiding the passage to the cellar. In the 1960s the cave suffered more serious roof falls which completely sealed the site.

With so many similarities with the St Nicholas Court site it is tempting to suggest that Nash Court cave was contemporary and of similar 14th century date.

The Shell Grotto, Margate

This intriguing Grade I listed site is located in Grotto Hill, Margate beneath urban housing and gardens and is a very popular tourist destination.

Since it was opened to the public in 1837 this distinctive underground structure has been the subject of much speculation and debate as to its origins. Many pamphlets, articles and papers have been written over the years, almost all of which concentrate their attention on the intricate patterns of shells which adorn the walls and roof and thus give the grotto its name.

The shell decoration consists of roughly square panels, each containing a specific design or motif with many of the designs incorporated in the

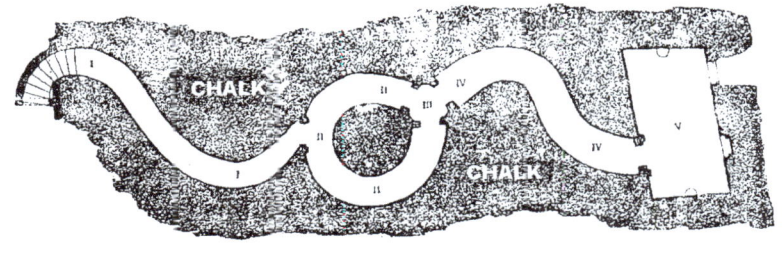

I. ENTRANCE II. ROTUNDA. III. THE DOME. IV. SERPENTINE PASSAGE. V. ALTAR CHAMBER

panels being sufficiently ambiguous to allow for several different explanations as to what they represent. It has been estimated that there are around 4.6 million shells covering 2000 square feet (186 square metres).

The interpretation of the symbolic meaning of the designs has lead to dates of Prehistoric, Roman, 18th century etc. proposed for the Grotto's construction and its purpose ranging from an ancient Phoenician temple, an early Masonic temple up to a 19th century folly.

Most of these theories are founded on hidden wisdom that is to be extracted from the layout of the shells.

Contemporary accounts regarding the discovery of the grotto vary but the common theme is that a spade was lost in a void when a cap-stone was disturbed in 1835. A small boy named Joshua, the young son of James Newlove, was lowered through the narrow hole on a length of rope to retrieve the tool. Newlove was the schoolmaster of the nearby boys' school, Dane House School.

The land above the site was later purchased by Newlove who opened the grotto to the public in 1837 after installing a horizontal entrance from the bottom of the hill and illuminating the tunnels with naked gas flame lighting.

The Grotto consists of three passages radiating from a narrow shaft known as the 'Dome'. One passage to the south leads to a roughly rectangular 'Altar' room whilst the other two curve round and join up to form the 'Rotunda'. A forth passage leads north from the 'Rotunda' and leads up to the surface via a set of modern steps.

All the walls of the structure apart from the entrance passage are covered with the shell decoration.

The writer's personal opinion is that a small medieval denehole type chalk mine could have been reworked and extended at some time after mining had ceased. The skill required to cut the passages to a relatively complex predetermined plan suggests that the date of the reworking could be from the 17th century onward although an 18th century date would seem more likely. It is probable that the shell decoration was undertaken at the same time or very shortly after.

Whoever commissioned and/or planned the elaborate designs for the shell panels was a well educated person who wove many different themes into the intricate patterns of literally millions of shells. At the time of writing historians are carrying out detailed research into contemporary documentary records which will hopefully add to our scant knowledge of this enigmatic structure.

It is highly likely that the Shell Grotto's original designer, whoever and whenever that was, has accomplished exactly what he set out to achieve i.e., speculation, controversy and conjecture which started with the discovery in 1835 and continues to the present day.

A fuller report on Margate Shell Grotto can be found on the Kent Archaeological Society's website.[27]

The Other Shell Grotto

It would perhaps be relevant to mention that a superficially similar structure to the Shell Grotto had been discovered thirty one years earlier near the High Street in Margate.

In 1804 both the Courier Magazine and The Times described a 'curious grotto' that had been discovered at Margate. Several writers, both past and present, have read the articles and have erroneously confused this site with that of the Shell Grotto. They are, in fact, completely separate structures and are of very different construction.

The earlier grotto was found during building work on the west side of Margate High Street on the premises of a Mr Oldfield who had a 25 year lease on a house which he converted into a boarding school. The Times article of 26th September 1804 describes the site as follows:

> "There is at Margate, although known to only a very few persons, a curious grotto, concerning the construction and real date of which nothing is certainly known. It is on the premises and behind the house of Mr Oldfield, and has a door which opens towards the sea, behind which is another, glazed with painted glass, on which are various well-executed emblematical representations, with two armorial bearings, and an inscription with the name of a Dutch lady and the date of 1612. Whether this is the date of its erection or not cannot precisely be told.
>
> The place is quadrangular, with a sort of wagon roof, and most plentifully adorned with valuable shells of various kinds and sizes. It is floored in compartments with smooth stones and the spaces in between filled with pebbles. In one corner is an antique earthenware vessel, seemingly intended for the holding of Holy Water, a conjecture which receives confirmation on the east side which appears to have been formed to represent an altar piece.
>
> There is, therefore, little or no doubt that this apartment was originally calculated for the most austere and sublime exercise of the Catholic Church, admitting no light but through the small stained window, which however, when opened, immediately discloses a view of the ocean. It is only within a short time that it has been discovered. Nobody knows, as far back as is recollected what the place contained: but it is said that it was the burial place of some old person who had once kept the house, on the site of which a seminary is now erected".

The site was incorporated into the cellars of the house which became known as Mrs Hill's Grotto House, Mrs Hill being the Landlord and owner of Grotto House and the adjacent Garden House.

At a later period the shell panels were removed and the site became a simple barrel vaulted cellar extension.

The house is still standing but has been renamed. It is still possible to discern the outline of the small window described above, although it has now been rendered over.

Chilton Farmhouse Tunnel

The 30m long tunnel that runs from the cellar of this 18th century building has been the subject of several published notes and articles over the years with much speculation as to its purpose. The passage, which lies approx. 8.0m below the surface, is rectangular in section and 1.8m high and 1.0m wide. At one point a bench has been cut in the side of the tunnel presumably for seating. As the tunnel proceeded away from the cellar, chalk spoil was removed via two shafts to the surface which were capped when digging finished, the one at the end being just inside the garden wall. The dog-legs and kinks in the passage suggest anti-blast protection and, together with the chalk bench, would perhaps indicate it was dug as a shelter. The size of the passages is similar to many World War One shelters in Thanet.

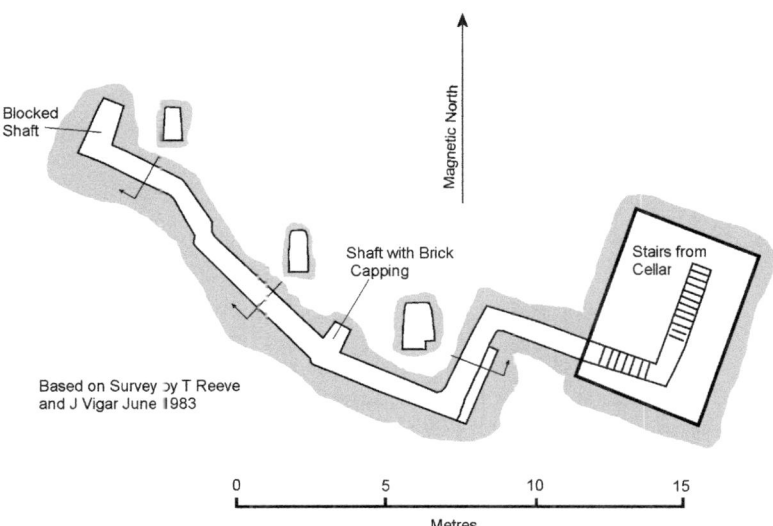

Smuggling Tunnels

It would be impossible to list all of the supposed smuggler's tunnels and caves that abound on the Island. Many tales of nefarious passages are based on hearsay passed down many generations with the story growing more and more questionable with each subsequent telling. There is usually, however, a small grain of truth in even the most implausible stories and it is certainly true that the 'free traders' used and adapted existing tunnels and caves for transportation and temporary storage. In a few cases they excavated new passages purely for their own use.

The Times newspaper of 19th January 1832 reported that officers of the Margate Custom House had searched a property occupied by a man named Cook *"…at the back of Zion Place near the Fort"'*. They discovered, hidden by a secret entrance, a tunnel which was: *"…just large enough to admit a man crawling upon his knees"*. The officers followed the sloping tunnel down towards the sea shore passing under several houses for about *"200 yards"* (183m) until they reached the lower entrance on the north-west side of Clifton Baths. This entrance was boarded over and had rammed earth and chalk covering it to conceal it from view. Inside the tunnel were found several wheeled trucks: *"…and implements for the conveying of smuggled goods through the tunnel to Cook's house."*

Apparently this was the second such tunnel that had been dug under the same house within two years.

Frank Illingworth's Tunnel, Pegwell Bay

An article, titled 'A Smuggler's Cave', was written by Frank Illingworth and published in the Kent County Journal for spring 1938 and describes the exploration of a tunnel at Pegwell Bay. Following directions from a local man, Illingworth and friends located a small tunnel about six feet (1.8m) up the cliff which they set out to explore using candles for illumination. After 200 yards (183m) of hands and knees crawling, a narrow blocked shaft was encountered leading up to the surface. After four hours of work clearing a way through the blockage at the base of the well-like shaft they continued on until the passage reduced in size to 2ft 6in (0.76m) wide and 22in (56cm) high with a chalk fall blocking the way forward. Following another five hours of toil, a 'room' and a tunnel leading towards the Lord of the Manor could be seen but the tunnel was now so narrow and the threat of roof falls so great that no further progress was attempted. During their digging an old pin-fire pistol was found along with three buttons said to be from an Exciseman's tunic.

In May 1983 the tunnel was relocated and surveyed by T Reeve and J Vigar and the plan published by the Chelsea Speleological Society.[28]

The total length of the accessible passage was found to be 175m, the well shaft described by Illingworth being 140m from the cliff entrance. The average size of the tunnel was 60cm high and 45cm wide with some parts only 35cm high. It was thought that the original height would have been about 1m but the floor was now covered by chalk debris. The shaft was of rough construction and was sealed with a wooden cover 3.5m

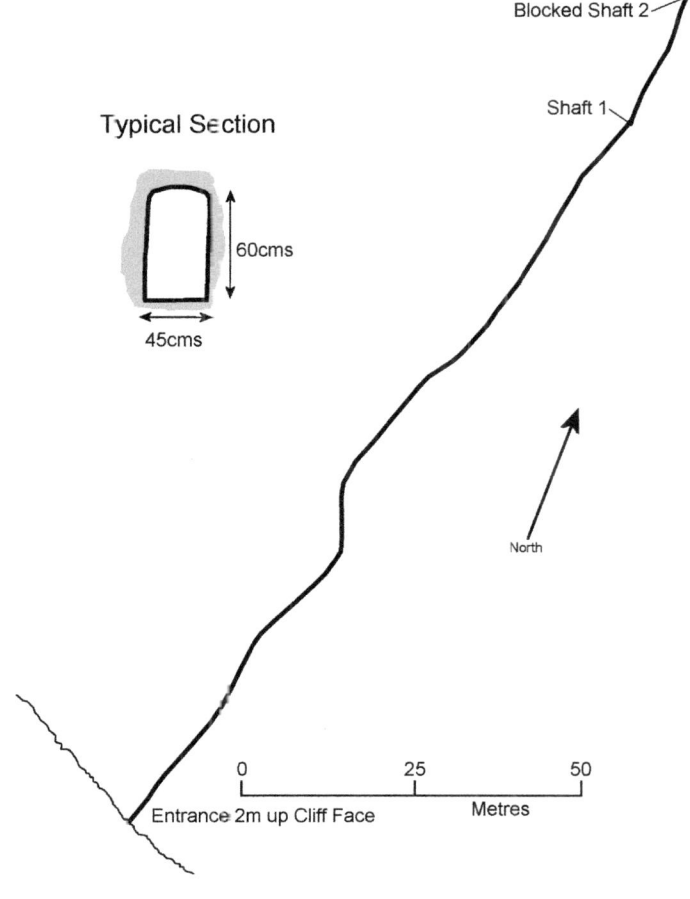

above the tunnel. Beyond the shaft the tunnel was of rougher construction and continued for another 20m until a major blockage now prevents further progress. This may be the site of another shaft or the 'domed room' described by Illingworth. This section was extremely tight and impossible to turn around in.

© *Vince Runacre*

Reeve and Vigar found much graffiti, mostly from the 1950s, but others beautifully cut, probably of 19th century date. The shaft and the blocked end of the tunnel are located in the grounds surrounding the site of an old cottage that was demolished around 1880 and it can be assumed that the tunnel was associated in some way with the property. It could be that the tunnel was dug simply as a drain to take effluent and rain run-off to discharge onto the sea shore. Along the tunnel at intervals in the roof are cylindrical holes 2.5cm in diameter which probably went up to the surface. These could have been used to keep the excavator on the correct alignment.

Whether the tunnel was dug by smugglers to move contraband from the shore to the environs of the old cottage, or dug as a practical way to get rid of waste is a matter of conjecture. The finding by Illingworth of the exciseman's buttons and the pistol would perhaps suggest it was used or at least suspected of being used for illicit purposes.

Extended Sea Caves

The chalk cliffs that form the coastline of Thanet have many natural caves formed by the action of the sea. Over time cracks and fissures in the chalk are enlarged by wave action and caverns are formed, some of considerable proportions.

It is beyond the scope of this small publication to list all such caves although most have been surveyed and recorded by KURG member Terry Reeve who has become the recognised expert in the surveying and recording of natural caves in the South-East.

Some of these naturally formed caves have been utilised by man over several centuries for the storage of fishing equipment, for shelter and the temporary storage of illicit cargoes.

In many cases a natural cave was enlarged or extended by the digging of other passages up to the cliff top.

Birchington

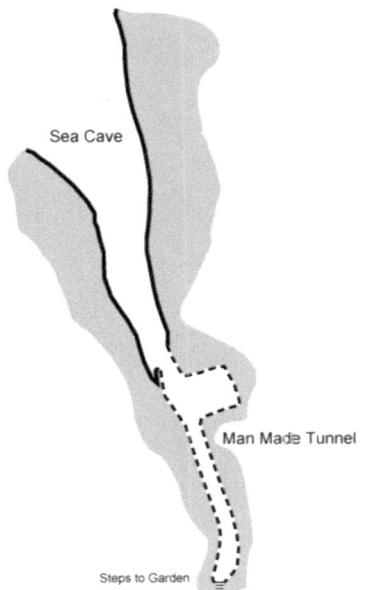

In a private garden backing onto the cliffs at Birchington, a flight of steps lead down to a wooden door which gives access to a steep man made tunnel that connects with an 11.6m long natural cave. This could be a classic example of a 'smuggler's cave' being a hidden way of bringing contraband from the beach to the cliff top.[29]

Captain Digby Tunnels, Kingsgate

In 1978 Terry Reeve surveyed some man made tunnels associated with a natural cave at Kingsgate. At the time known locally as the 'Smugglers Cave' or 'Joss Snelling's Cave' after the notorious local smuggler, they extend beneath the rear garden of the Captain Digby Hotel. (TR 396 708) Terry describes the site as:

> *"A passage 10ft wide and 30ft high (3m by 9.1m) runs for 150ft (45.7m) where a pile of debris blocks the tunnel and could mark the position of a filled shaft to the surface. About halfway along the cave another passage branches off at a right angle to a second entrance 15ft (4.6m) above the beach.'*
>
> *To what extent the cave is natural is uncertain, though it would seem that everything beyond the 65ft (18.8m) long wave cut channel in the main entrance has probably been dug."* [30]

Some time later a subsidence occurred in the car park of the Hotel which was probably caused by the settling and further roof collapse at the site of the blockage mentioned above.

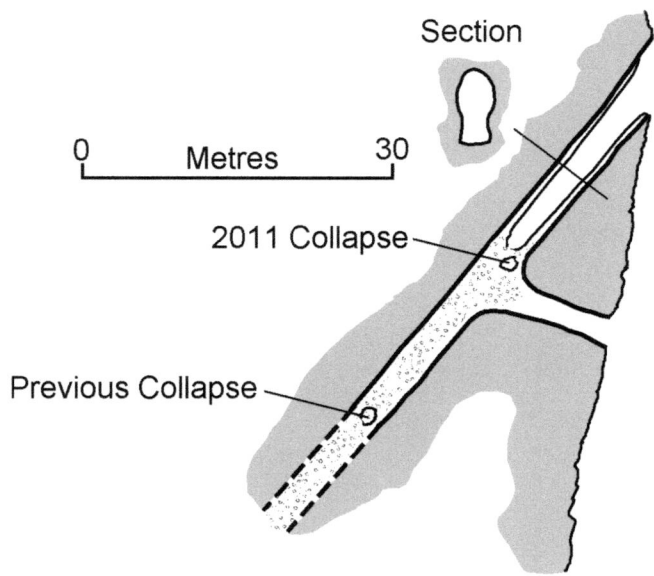

In 2011 the caves were re-examined by KURG members following a subsidence which affected a footpath near the corner of a children's play area. The collapse occurred when the roof of the passage fell in, probably the result of a leaking pipe which had saturated the chalk strata resulting in a catastrophic failure of the roof or a blocked shaft. During the brief assessment of the cave, the site of the previous collapse was noted, where the remedial action taken appears to have been the construction of a rough containment barrier made of concrete posts inside the cave, which holds back chalk rubble and debris. On the surface a shingle feature marks the site.

Cartographic evidence indicates that the tunnel continues in a straight line from the site of the subsidences towards the south-west corner of the original property boundary. An undated estate plan shows the line of the tunnel which is marked as 'Tunnel to the Beach'.

Large scale Ordnance Survey plans of the site dated between 1871 and 1890 also mark the site of the tunnel, delineating it with a pair of pecked lines. The Ordnance Survey plans also show what must have been the sloping entrance to the tunnel at the south-west end.

Between 1763 and 1768 Lord Holland constructed a 'Bede House' for entertaining the visitors who came to see his celebrated follies. By 1809 it became known as 'The Noble Captain Digby'. Most of the modern Captain Digby dates from the early 19th century as a large part of the original Bede House fell into the sea during an exceptionally bad storm in 1816.

Although it is highly possible that the tunnel to the beach was in existence before the Bede House was constructed it is more likely that it was excavated around the same time to give the visitors easy access to the beach below. It is also probable that the short branch tunnel was dug at this time.[31]

Whiteness Cave, Kingsgate

At Whiteness Point a natural sea cave 20.7m long has had an additional 54.3m of man made tunnels added. An opening in Whiteness gap, now bricked up, leads to a passage over 36m long which terminates in an opening in the cliff 4.6m up from the beach. About 22.9m along the passage a second tunnel runs south to a similar lookout position above the beach.[32]

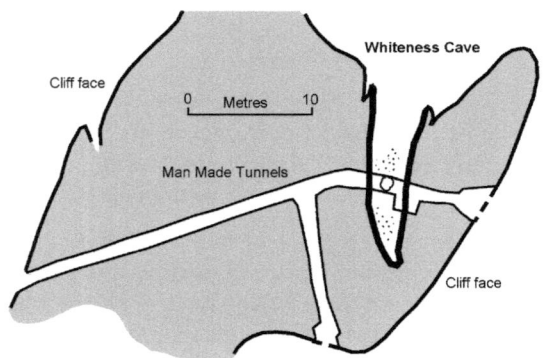

Pegwell Bay

In 1970, Harry Pearman of KURG visited Pegwell Bay in order to find and survey Frank Illingworth's tunnel. He was unsuccessful in locating that particular feature but did record some man made tunnels at TR 365 641. Two entrances, one at ground level and the other about 3m up the cliff, led to around 76m of tunnels with an arched cross section, on average 1.6m in height and 1.2m wide. The tunnels are known locally as 'The Witches' Kitchen'.[33]

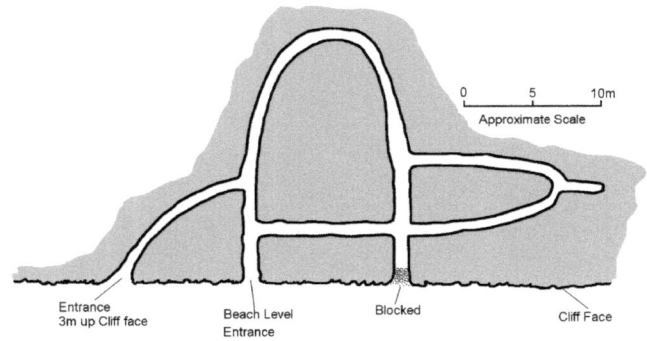

Another interesting set of tunnels dug from a sea cave at Pegwell Bay was recorded by Terry Reeve in 1997.[34]

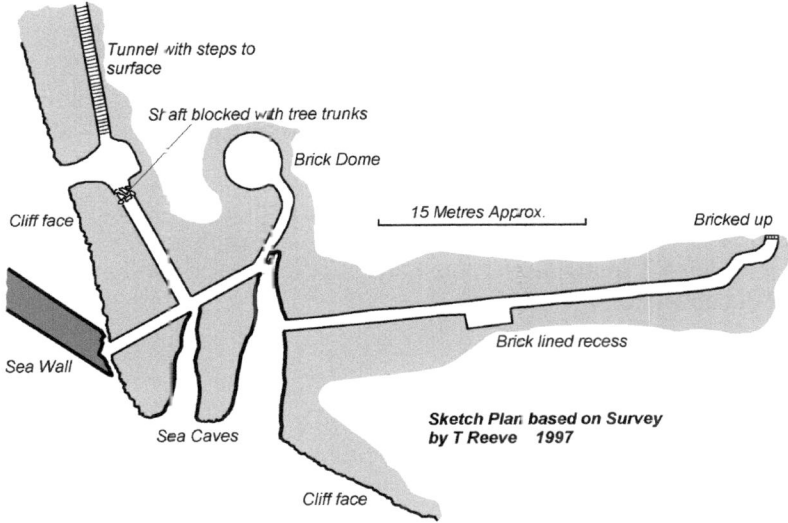

He writes:

> "More tunnels can be entered near the eastern end of the sea wall. One steeply ascending passage, with steps cut in the floor, has not been fully examined due to lack of light. Another tunnel, about 60ft (18.3m) long, connects with a large sea cave that lies just around the corner from the Bay. Two more passages lead off from the sea cave: a tunnel extending eastwards for several hundred feet is terminated by brickwork: and another about 40ft (12.2m) long terminates in a small chamber with a brick dome in the roof."

The tunnels are known as the Blockhouse Caves.

The Future of Underground Thanet

All the caves and tunnels mentioned in this short paper are probably only a fraction of those that have been dug out over the course of hundreds of years.

For safety reasons underground sites are filled, entrances bricked up and otherwise made safe. The action of tides and weather erode the chalk cliffs containing caves and man made passages causing them to collapse and block the entrances.

Undoubtedly, however, other previously unknown sites will be discovered in the future as building works, landscaping etc. disturb the capping of old shafts or entrances and reveal new sites to be recorded and documented.

Appendix

List of proposed dug outs in Margate during First World War.

Dear Sir,

I beg to inform you that the watch committee acting on the instructions of the Borough Council have decided to construct an adequate number of dug-outs in all parts of the Borough for Sheltering the public during hostile air raids.

I feel quite sure that the pressing necessity there is in the town at the present time for such accommodation needs no words of mine to command your aid. I therefore venture to ask if you will give them all the help you can afford so that these places can be started upon at once and completed in the least possible time as it is impossible to procure the necessary paid labour, and the urgent need brooks no delay.

Kindly inform me as soon as possible what service you can give as it is desirable to enlist the services of all the men folk in the town to give a hand in this work, and to make the best possible use of them I propose that each volunteer shall be detailed to a site that is most convenient to him, and in accordance with the numbers they will be divided up in shift relays in such a way that the work will be rarely stopped until completed.

Yours faithfully,

Alfred Appleyard.

Chief Constable.

LIST OF PLACES WHERE IT IS PROPOSED TO CONSTRUCT DUG-OUTS

Wilderness Hill.	Hawley Square gardens
Moore's Laundry, Dane Road.	Milton and Byron Roads
Lower Northdown Road.	Ramsgate Road
Madiera Road.	Tivoli Green
Northdown Road. (Opposite Hill's Butchers)	Buckingham Road
Northdown Road. (Opposite Lloyds Bank)	Alexandra Road
Victoria Avenue (Corporation Land)	College Road
Newgate Gapway	Frog Hill
Land opposite Palladium	Hawley Street
Sewer Dane Road	New Cross Street Schools
Clifton Baths	Margate Brewery Vaults
Ball Room Queen's Hotel	Corporation Yard King Street
Vortigen Caves	Trinity Square
Marine Terrace Green	
Sea View Terrace	
Westbrook Bathing Pavilion	

End Notes

1. Archaeologia Cantiana Vol. XI 1877 p126-127
2. The Ingoldsby Legends by Thomas Ingoldsby (The Rev. Richard H. Barham) London, Bentley 1840 p328
3. Archaeologia Cantiana CXXV 2005 p393
4. KURG Research Report 12 1995 p11
5. KURG Research Report 8 1992 p7-8
6. KURG Newsletter 103 2011 p6-7
7. CSS Records volume 6 1974 p37 also KURG Newsletter 99 2009 p1-2
8. CSS Records volume 23 1997 p23 plan p25 also Isle of Thanet Gazette for 15th November 1984
9. Bygone Kent Volume 3 No 8 1982
10. Thanet in Wartime by J T Huddlestone (Chairman of Ramsgate ARP Committee) Published in instalments in the Thanet Gazette. 'Thanet Troglodytes' Chapter VIII 14th June 1938
11. KURG Newsletter 92 2007 p3-4
12. KURG Newsletter 101 2010 p1-3
13. KURG Research Report 11 1994 p19
14. KURG Research Report 12 1995 p1-2
15. KURG Newsletter 98 2009 p3-5
16. KURG Newsletter 92 2007 p1-3
17. KURG Newsletter 83 2004 p2-3
18. KURG Newsletter 95 2008 p1-4
19. KURG Research Report 11 1994 p22 also Bygone Kent vol. 30 no1 2009
20. KURG Research Report 8 1992 p18-20
21. Combined Kent Underground Research Group Annual Report 2002/3 and Chelsea Speleological Society Records Volume 31 pp6-13 2004
22. KURG Research Report 11 1994 p24-28
23. Excavations of an Iron Age Pit and Roman Cave at Manston in the Isle of Thanet Colin A Baker 2010 (Available from the Trust for Thanet Archaeology)
24. Current Archaeology 101, p167-168 1986
25. Archaeologia Cantiana vol. CXXI 2001 p367.
26. Subterranea Britannica Bulletin No 15 1982 p14-15
27. www.kentarchaeology.ac/authors/023.pdf
28. Chelsea Speleological Society Newsletter vol.25 no7 1983 also CSS Records vol. 6 p56 1974
29. Chelsea Speleological Society Records vol.9 p11 1979
30. Chelsea Speleological Society Records vol.9 p12 1979
31. KURG Annual Report 2011/12 p30-31
32. Chelsea Speleological Society Records vol.9 p15 1979
33. Chelsea Speleological Society Records vol.6 p59 1974
34. Chelsea Speleological Society Records vol.23 p45 1997

Further Study

For a comprehensive history of the Ramsgate World War Two Shelters, *Ramsgate Has the World's Finest Shelters* by Phil Spain is obtainable from the Ramsgate Tunnels website at £4.99 [post free] or Michael's Bookshop 72, King Street, Ramsgate (personal callers only).

For information on the top secret Home Guard Auxillary Units, *The Last Ditch* by David Lampe 2007 (Greenhill Books ISBN 978-1-85367-730-4), and *With Britain in Mortal Danger* edited by John Warwicker MBE 2002 (Cerberus Publishing ISBN 1-84145-112-6).

Useful Websites

www.thanetarch.co.uk The Trust for Thanet Archaeology's official website.

www.kurg.org.uk The Kent Underground Research Group' site.

www.iotas.org.uk The Isle of Thanet Archaeological Society's site.

www.undergroundkent.co.uk Run by a KURG member many photos and background information on sites in Kent and the south-east.

http://thanetundergroundblogspot.com Run by a KURG member concentrating on sites on the Isle of Thanet.

www.shellgrotto.co.uk The Shell Grotto official web site.

www.margatecaves.co.uk for latest information on the Margate Caves and the campaign to have them re-opened to the public.

www.ramsgatetunnels.org for information on the Ramsgate ARP shelters and the attempts to have part of them open for public access.

www.subbrit.org.uk A national society devoted to man made underground features with a large collection of photos of Kent sites including Thanet.

www.kentarchaeology.ac The Kent Archaeological Society's website which features two Thanet sites in its e-articles section: The Shell Grotto and Margate Caves.

Index

Abbey School, 66
Acol, 15
Addington Square, Margate, 37
Albion Road, St Peters, 26
Alland Grange, 16, 38-40
Anvil Close, Birchington, 25
Auxiliary Units, Home Guard, 55-56

Basford, Hazel, 17, 23
Bede House, 78
Birchington
    Anvil Close, 25
    Quex Park, 16-17, 23
    Smuggler's Cave, 77
Blockhouse Caves, Pegwell Bay, 80
Brazier, 19
Brewery Vaults, Margate, 30
Buchan, John, 57
Bush Farm, Manston, 11

Captain Digby Hotel, Kingsgate, 77
Captain Digby Tunnels, 77,-78
Chalk
    Chalk Extraction, 9
    Chalk for Agriculture, 10
    Chalk for Brickmaking, 26-29
    Chalk for Lime burning, 13-25
Chatham Street, Ramsgate, 32-34
Cheesemans Farm, 38
Chelsea Speleological Society, 74
Chilton Farmhouse Tunnel, Pegwell, 72
Chislehurst Caves, 22
Clarendon House Grammar School, 36
Clifton Baths, Margate, 30, 73
Cliftonville
    Eastern Esplanade, 57
    Northdown Park Road, 30-32
    Wishing Towers Hotel, 57-58
Custom House, Margate, 73

Dane House School, 69
Drapers Mill School, 36
East Cliff Caverns, Ramsgate, 61
East Cliff, Ramsgate, 53-54, 61
Eastern Esplanade, Cliftonville, 57
Ellington School, Ramsgate, 34-36
Elmwood Avenue, Kingsgate, 13
Enigmatic Sites, 63-72
Extended Sea Caves, 76-81
Fervent, HMS, Ramsgate, 53-55
Flint House, Margate, 22
Flint Row, Margate, 22, 24
Foad, Suzannah, 31
Forster, Francis, 18, 19
Frank Illingworth's Tunnel, 73-75, 79

Gardner, James Geary, 22
Grange The, Ramsgate, 30, 39, 59-61
Granville Caves, Ramsgate, 61-62
Gravett, Ken, 64
Grotto House, Mrs Hill's, 71

Hill, Mrs, Grotto House, 71
HMS Fervent, Ramsgate, 53-55
Holland, Lord, 78
Hollowcombe Down, Ramsgate, 9
Holy Trinity Church, Margate, 20, 22
Home Guard Auxiliary Units, 55-56

Illingworth, Frank, 73, 75, 79
Ingoldsby Legends, 11
Isle of Thanet Archaeological Society, 24

King George VI Park, Ramsgate, 61
Kingsgate
    Captain Digby Hotel, 77
    Quarry Tunnels, 13
    Whiteness Cave, 79

Lambert, P.J.C, 64

Lord Holland, 78
Lord of the Manor, Ramsgate, 73
Luff, S.G.A, 66
Lydden, 55

Manston, 10
Manston
    Airfield, 38, 55
    Caves, 10-12
    Bush Farm, 11
    Shelter, 46-48
    Spratling Court Farm, 63
    Underground Hangars, 39

Margate
    Addington Square, 37
    Brewery vaults, 30
    Caves, 17-22, 30
    Clifton Baths, 30, 73
    Custom House, 73
    Flint House, 22
    Flint Row, 22, 24
    High Street, 70
    Holy Trinity Church, 20, 22
    Other Shell Grotto, 70-71
    School of Art, 22
    Shell Grotto, 67-70
    Zion Place, 21, 73

McIntosh, K.H, 64
Miles, Andy, 13, 52

Nash Court, 55, 65
Nash Court Cave, 65-67
Newlove, James, 69
North Foreland, 57
Northdown, 10
Northdown Hill, St Peters, 28-29
Northdown Park Road, Cliftonville, 30-31
Northumberland Fusiliers, 36
Northumberland House, 18-20, 22
Norwood, John, 19

Oldfield, Mr, 70, 71
Other Shell Grotto, Margate, 70-71

Paragon Shelter, Ramsgate, 30
Parfitt, Keith, 63
Pearman, Harry, 79
Pegwell Bay, 79, 80
Pegwell Bay
    Chilton Farmhouse Tunnel, 72
    Seaweed Tunnel, 8
    Witches Kitchen, 79
Perkins Dave, 28
Pouce's Farm, 38
Prior, Dr, 20
Pugin, Augustus, 59, 61

Quex Park, Birchington, 16-17, 23

Ramsgate, 9
Ramsgate
    Chatham Street, 32-34
    Deep ARP Shelters, 40-44
    East Cliff, 53-54, 61
    East Cliff Caverns, 61
    Ellington School, 34-36
    Granville Caves, 61
    HMS Fervent, 53-55
    Hollowcombe Down (Hollicondane), 9
    King George VI Park, 61
    Lord of the Manor, 73
    Paragon Shelter, West Cliff, 30
    Rank Flour Mills, 44-46
    Six Mile Mine, 13
    The Grange, 30, 39, 59-61
    West Cliff, 30
Reeve, T, 74, 75, 76, 77, 80
Reeve's Brickfield, 10, 29
Runacre, Angie, 38, 39

Sarre, Battle HQ, 52-53
Scott, Rev. WA, 65
Seaweed Tunnel, Pegwell Bay, 8

Shell Grotto, Margate, 67-70
Six Mile Mine, Ramsgate, 13
Smuggler Bill, 11
Smuggling Tunnels 73-75
Spain, Phil, 44
Spratling Court Farm, Manston, 63
St Cuby, 57
St Nicholas at Wade
    Underground Chapel, 64-65
    St Nicholas Court, 64
St Peters, 10
St Peters
    High Street, 49
    Albion Road, 26
    Northdown Hill, 28
    Victoria Road, 30
Steed, Norman, 55

Thanet at War, 30-56
'The 39 Steps', 57
Transport, 57-62
Troward, William, 10, 11

Underground Chapel, St Nicholas at Wade, 64- 65
Underground Hangars, Manston, 39

Vigar, J, 74, 75
Vincent Farm, 38

Wells, Paul, 13, 38, 52
West Cliff, Ramsgate, 30
Whissen, R, 37
Whiteness Cave, Kingsgate, 79
Wishing Towers Hotel, Cliftonville, 57-59
Witches Kitchen, Pegwell Bay, 79

Zion Place, Margate, 21, 73

The Trust for Thanet Archaeology is a charitable trust that provides professional archaeological services to developers, educational activities to the community and hosts an excellent web site which includes a Virtual Museum of Thanet's Archaeology. (www.thanetarch.co.uk)

The Trust has a full time Director and Deputy Director and works with the assistance of professional field archaeologists as well as volunteers from the local archaeological society and undergraduate archaeology students.

The Kent Underground Research Group was formed in 1981 to carry out research into the origins, use and history of the many subterranean features of Kent and the South East.

The members are a unique mixture of the practical and academic. On the active side they explore and survey underground features for which they have the necessary skills and equipment. Some projects call for technical expertise in the use of pumps, winches, timbering, etc. Safety is a very big feature in the Group's activities and new members are taught the skills by others with many years' experience. On the academic side, they carry out research into old records as well as talking to elderly residents whose memories are invaluable. (www.kurg.org.uk)